More Praise for
The Accidental Entrepreneur

"*The Accidental Entrepreneur* is jam-packed with practical tools, powerful insights and clear-cut strategies that will take you and your business to the next level. Susan Urquhart-Brown uses her passion and incredible marketing savvy to show you how to become an entrepreneur on purpose. This book is a must read!"

—Andrea Frank Henkart, Psy.D.(c),
best-selling author, *Cool Communication*

"*The Accidental Entrepreneur* is an absolute MUST for anyone dreaming of becoming an entrepreneur. This step-by-step guide can turn that dream into a successful reality."

—Susan Ireland, owner, Susan Ireland Résumés

The Accidental Entrepreneur

Things I Wish Someone Had Told Me About Starting a Business

SUSAN URQUHART-BROWN

AMERICAN MANAGEMENT ASSOCIATION
New York • Atlanta • Brussels • Chicago • Mexico City • San Francisco
Shanghai • Tokyo • Toronto • Washington, D.C.

Special discounts on bulk quantities of AMACOM books are available to corporations, professional associations, and other organizations. For details, contact Special Sales Department, AMACOM, a division of American Management Association, 1601 Broadway, New York, NY 10019.
Tel.: 212-903-8316.   Fax: 212-903-8083.
E-mail: specialsls@amanet.org
Website: www.amacombooks.org/go/specialsales
To view all AMACOM titles go to: www.amacombooks.org

This publication is designed to provide accurate and authoritative information in regard to the subject matter covered. It is sold with the understanding that the publisher is not engaged in rendering legal, accounting, or other professional service. If legal advice or other expert assistance is required, the services of a competent professional person should be sought.

Library of Congress Cataloging-in-Publication Data

Urquhart-Brown, Susan.
    The accidental entrepreneur : 50 things I wish someone had told me about starting a business / Susan Urquhart-Brown.
        p.   cm.
    Includes index.
    ISBN-13: 978-0-8144-0167-5
    ISBN-10: 0-8144-0167-8
    1. Self-employed—Handbooks, manuals, etc.   2. New business enterprises—United States—Management—Handbooks, manuals, etc.
    3. New business enterprises—Management—Handbooks, manuals, etc.
    4. Self-employed—United States—Handbooks, manuals, etc.
    5. Entrepreneurship—Handbooks, manuals, etc.   I. Title.

HD8037.U5U77   2008
658.1'1—dc22

                                                        2008008102

Printing number

10   9   8   7   6   5   4   3   2   1

Contents

CHAPTER THREE
TAKING CARE OF BUSINESS

CHAPTER FOUR
WHAT DO YOU BRING TO THE PARTY?

CHAPTER FIVE
MARKET AND SELL YOUR SOCKS OFF!

CHAPTER SIX
GET CONNECTED TO THE WEB FOR PROFIT

CHAPTER SEVEN
MAKING ROOM FOR MORE BUSINESS

Foreword by Jim Horan

Going solo is difficult . . . even for the best and strongest of entrepreneurs. The emotional ups and downs can be significant. In *The Accidental Entrepreneur: 52 Things I Wish Someone Had Told Me about Starting a Business*, Susan Urquhart-Brown speaks powerfully to the interpersonal aspects of self-employment as well as the practical nuts and bolts. Sometimes she offers a pep talk, encouraging you to try something new and bold. Other times, she gives a dose of "tough love" to get you back on track.

From my experience, I know that the author is someone who has not only walked her talk, but understands the people side of entrepreneurship, and that her advice is practical and real as well as inspiring. This guidebook is the result of lessons the Author learned over the past 12 years of building her business and coaching successful entrepreneurs like myself.

Business theory doesn't get your phone to ring. ***The Accidental Entrepreneur*** leaves the theory behind and clearly spells out a roadmap to guide you from being an accidental entrepreneur to an intentional entrepreneur with a thriving business. This guidebook is sure to become a well-worn companion on your desk. Susan made sure that each bite-size section is on-point, a quick read, and immediately actionable.

Good ideas are a dime a dozen. The value is in implementation. If you are considering entrepreneurship, this book contains easy exercises and a reality check to determine if it is a good fit for you. If you have a business that's ready for the next level, this book is filled with marketing and sales tips designed to move your business way beyond "just getting by." Susan also includes the wisdom gained from over 20 successful entrepreneurs as they share those things they wish someone had told them before they started their business!

One of the nice things about this book is that it is written by an entrepreneur for entrepreneurs; it is written in simple, clear, understandable language. It is also very easy to find real, practical solutions to the problems you are struggling with because the book is organized either around solutions . . . or problems. For example,

- Why and how procrastination can be good

- Working through self-sabotage and resistance

- Five secrets of marketing your business

- Six ways to differentiate your business

- Your 30-second elevator speech

- A system to help make your networking payoff

- Four ways to use customer service as a sales and retention tool

- How to handle a demanding customer

- Warming up to cold calling

- Six ways to promote your business via the web

And it doesn't matter if you own or want to start a professional practice, a service company, sell insurance, real estate, or even a product . . . *The Accidental Entrepreneur* will begin to change your life and your business from the day you open it!

Who can benefit from reading this book? You can.

• If you are currently employed and considering starting a small business, *The Accidental Entrepreneur* will help you clearly decide whether self-employment is a good fit for you.

• If you do decide to venture forth and start a business, *The Accidental Entrepreneur* will help you here, too. The advice it gives is practical and proven. This is the best guidebook you could possibly buy.

• If you already own a small business and are ready to take it to the next level, the marketing and sales tips Susan shares in this book can really turbocharge your business!

• If you are a professional coach, consultant, or professor, you will want this book in your library—and it should be required reading for your clients or students as well.

Unfortunately, far too many books on entrepreneurship are written by people who never started or built a business of their own. I've watched Susan build her business over the last twelve years. This book shares not only what worked but also what didn't. Both aspects are equally important.

Thanks to Susan's advice (and an occasional kick in the butt), we have built The One Page Business Plan Company into a global "best practices company," complete with books, seminars, workshops, and software.

Best wishes for building an incredibly successful business!

—Jim Horan (another Accidental Entrepreneur)

Acknowledgments

To Christopher, Christian, and Kevin Brown, and my many friends and colleagues who encouraged me along the way!

Special thanks to the entrepreneurs profiled in this book, who shared their wisdom, insights, stories, and practical tips to inspire others along the entrepreneurial path.

Introduction

WHAT IS AN "accidental entrepreneur"? The answer is: a person who never expected to be self-employed or thought of herself or himself as an entrepreneur.

An accidental entrepreneur is not a born or natural entrepreneur, or even someone who is comfortable, at first, selling products or services. Accidental entrepreneurs don't set out to be entrepreneurs; rather, they find themselves working on their own by chance or reluctant choice, and only gradually come to find that they enjoy it. At that point, they realize that they need to learn what they don't already know—everything they can, in fact—in order to make their business a success.

Here are a few examples of accidental entrepreneurs:

• A communication specialist takes a retirement package, and a few months later she agrees to do a project for her former boss. The boss, enthused about the specialist's work, recommends her to someone in another company. Soon she is working on projects for three companies. One day it dawns on her that she has a consulting business. This is fine with her. But so far this work came strictly through referrals. How can she market herself to other companies?

• An engineer has not been able to find work in the high-tech industry and needs money to pay his mortgage. He takes a substitute-teaching job at a local school and discovers that many of his students need tutoring in math. He starts an after-school tutoring program and discovers that he really enjoys working with students, especially those who are math-phobic. He realizes that he could build a business around this. But how?

• A therapist, counselor, or coach finds herself enjoying working one-on-one with clients and wants to build a private practice. She keeps her "day job" while slowly developing a referral base. At some point, she knows she wants to do this work full-time, but she doesn't have enough clients to support herself to this degree. What steps does she need to take in order to accomplish this goal?

• A corporate refugee has a vision of living a quieter life, away from the city and the long commute. She manages to move with her husband to a small tourist town. However, this new area offers very few well-paying jobs. The couple realize that they need to make their living on their own, and decide to open a gift store, although neither of them has any retail experience. They decide to invest their savings in this store. What do they need to learn in order to make the store a moneymaker and to keep its doors open over time?

In all these cases, and many more like them, the decision to be an entrepreneur comes about gradually, as events change, priorities shift, and the need to make a living creates new needs and new possibilities. In almost every one of these cases, there's a lot to consider before just jumping in, if the business is to get off the ground and keep on going.

Passion and motivation are the first considerations. Entrepreneurship is like running a marathon. You might run to lose weight, to get in shape, to prove you can do it, or for a cause. These are all good reasons. But do they have sticking power? Is your heart really in it? Before you take your first running step, it would help to ask yourself, "Why am I doing this?" If your answer is, "Because I'm enthusiastic and passionate about it," then you will have a good chance. When your heart is truly connected with your goal, then you are willing to train, to run, to move past your obstacles, to reach the finish line, and to celebrate your success—and then do it all over again! (The next time, however, you can learn from your mistakes and get to the finish line faster).

You may begin your entrepreneurial career by accident, but it's important to make this move intentional as soon as possible. For only once it becomes intentional will you give your business the kind of care it needs, and make it possible for it to give back to you the kind of profit and enjoyment you hoped for in the first place.

Being an entrepreneur is far more creative than doing a job for someone else. Your business is a reflection of who you are and what you're passionate about, as well as the unique expertise you have to offer the marketplace. If you are a sole proprietor—or, as I like to say, a "SoloPreneur"—you make all the decisions, you do most of the work, you solve the problems, you take the heat when things go wrong, and you bask in the glory when things go right. It's exciting and scary, but you are doing what you love.

How to Use This Book

I wrote this book so that everyone whose heart's desire is to have a successful business has the opportunity to create, sustain, and grow the business that best fits their expertise, passion, and the needs of their perfect clients or customers. This book is for entrepreneurs who have from zero to twenty employees.

This book will boost your confidence and give you the tools and techniques to reach your goals, one step at a time, as well as stories and practical tips from entrepreneurs who have taken the leap and have successful businesses! The book can be digested in bite-sized pieces. Look at the table of contents, then turn to the section that interests you most. Read one whole section at one sitting, or just read one chapter. Do one exercise. Prioritize the ideas, tools, or techniques that fit your business strategies and that you would like to implement. Apply the ideas directly to your business. Then add them to your action-item list or business plan.

In other words, this book is designed to be useful, practical, accessible, and encouraging, and, most of all, to guide you from being an accidental entrepreneur to being an intentional entrepreneur with a thriving business.

CHAPTER 1

WHAT IS AN ENTREPRENEUR, ANYWAY?

Eight Questions to Ask Before You Start a Business

HAVE YOU BEEN THINKING about making your endeavor into a business? Are you confused about where to start and what to do? If you answered yes, your next move is to answer the following questions for yourself. This will help you to gain the clarity needed to find direction. Also, the thinking and research you do as you answer these questions will become your steps for starting your business. Don't be like 95 percent of wannabe entrepreneurs who think they have a great idea and jump into business without careful planning. Some people who follow this strategy are very successful; but if you look before you leap, your percentage for success will be much higher.

Questions to Ask Yourself

1. *"Who am I?"* Starting and running a business is a lot like running a marathon. There will be highs and lows, and the prospect is both exciting and scary. To maximize your chances, analyze your strengths and weaknesses as well as your personal characteristics. For example, to be in business, you need determination, persistence, creativity, flexibility, and a steep learning curve. Will you be able to develop and strengthen these characteristics better by

> **1** *"Don't be like 95 percent of wannabe entrepreneurs who think they have a great idea and jump into business without careful planning."*

working alone, being in a partnership, or being at the helm of a fast-growing organization? How does your business idea fit in with your personal goals for the next three to five years? Your business idea, your expertise, and your personality all need to fit well with the type of company you're growing.

2. *"What business am I in?"* Carefully define and detail what your product and/or services are. What problems do you solve? What benefits do you provide? Who are you targeting to buy your services? Consumers? Organizations? Where are they located? How will you reach them? For example, if you want to build a coaching practice, what type of coaching do you offer—executive coaching in which your clients are corporations, or personal coaching in which your clients are individuals? Learn everything you can about the business you want to start and the marketplace in which you plan to operate.

3. *"Is my business idea viable?"* In order to find out, market research is essential so that you can answer such questions as, "Who will buy my product?" and "Are there enough potential customers out there for me to make a profit?" Identify and analyze what your competitors are doing, and how what you offer is sufficiently different to attract customers. But you don't need to do expensive focus groups. You can test market your idea with a group of friends and colleagues; interview competitors who are willing to talk to you; and research your industry and the market trends via the Internet or the local library. Other resources are the Small Business Administration Resource Centers, your local Chamber of Commerce, and successful entrepreneurs in a business related to yours.

4. *"What is my market niche?"* What is unique about you and your business? What do you want to be known for? If you fit your niche well, even in a recession, people will ask first about your product or service, and second about price. *Hint*: Having a niche does not mean offering the lowest price. Any competitor can charge less. A market niche is what makes your business stand out from the pack. However, any old niche won't work. It has to be one that is focused, or narrow, but deep—that is, having enough potential customers in your targeted niche to bring you the business volume you want that will make your business profitable. For example, publishing companies are creating more specialty magazines. There is even one called *Prison Life*, which has a specialized but huge captive audience—literally.

5. *"How will I market my business?"* The marketing strategies you choose must do two things: One, reach your target customers, and two, fit your business because you must continually market your business. Out of sight (or sound) is out of mind. For example, speaking and writing is a good marketing mix for business consultants. Back-of-the-room sales are also brisk if you have authored a book. However, if you love to give talks but you own a retail store, your store location and a well-placed radio or TV/cable commercial might reach a wider audience of potential customers.

6. *"How will I finance my business?"* The flip side of the question, "Will I make enough money?" is "Do I have enough money to get started?" Work with an accountant or business consultant to carefully determine how much start-up funding you need and help you do a profit-and-loss projection. I recommend that you have enough personal funds to finance your living expenses for your first year of business. If you get a business loan, remember that you must put up collateral, which is often your house; if you get financing from angel investors, you must give up equity in your business, which may mean you won't have control over what your business really is and how you run it.

7. *"Why do I need a business plan?"* Now that you've decided to go into business and you have done your research, you are ready to write a business plan. Planning ahead can mean the difference between success and failure. This is the stage when you get your ideas out of your head and onto paper. You set your goals for the year, as well as strategies and specific plans for how you'll reach your goals. The written plan is a document that you can use to quickly explain your business to potential investors and—more importantly—to keep yourself on track.

8. *"Will I go into my own business?"* Are you going to run the marathon? Answering the above questions carefully will help you make a well-informed decision. If you're ready, start running now. Remember: Even though there are obstacles along the way, a marathon always has a well-planned course to follow.

Myths About Going into Business for Yourself

SOMETIMES A PERSON decides to go solo on a whim, based on some common myths about the joys of working for oneself. If you're considering starting a business, review the following common myths before you decide to proceed, so that you can avoid the pitfalls that go along with them:

• *Myth 1: "I'll try it out and see how it goes."* Many people who are between jobs decide it's as good a time as any to start a business. However, choosing to go solo by default is not a wise idea. Starting a business is very demanding and includes long working hours, financial investment, and, of course, no regular paycheck. It is not something to go into lightly. If all you are doing is "Trying It Out," it's bound to fail. Don't waste your time and money.

• *Myth 2: "When I'm my own boss, I'll avoid corporate politics."* Just because you're the boss doesn't mean you don't have anyone to answer to. You will have many more bosses than you ever did as an employee—bosses called "customers," "corporations," or "investors." So instead of dealing with the politics of a single company, you may have to handle the politics of twenty companies. It's up to you to stay tuned into the needs and subtleties of each company and figure out how to meet those needs if you want to continue to be retained.

> **2** *"Just because you're the boss doesn't mean you don't have anyone to answer to. You will have many more bosses than you ever did as an employee."*

• *Myth 3: "I'll have more free time and flexible work hours."* If you think you will have time to spend on your hobbies, play tennis a couple days a week, and schedule time off whenever you want, think again. The first few years you will most likely spend sixty to eighty hours per week getting your business up and running. Moreover, the number of hours you spend working for yourself is not likely to lessen as your business grows. In addition to spending time delivering your service, you will be marketing your services, running your business, doing paperwork, solving problems, and developing new products and services. Be realistic about how many hats you have to wear as a business owner and how much time it really takes to get everything done. One client of mine said, "Yes, I have flexible hours. I can work until 2 A.M.!"

• *Myth 4: "All I need is a good idea."* There are many wonderful ideas and products that have never seen the light of day. It's much easier to come up with ideas than to implement them. However, even if you follow through with building the better mousetrap, your business may not succeed. Even if you have a good idea and the technical expertise to create the product, you also need to be able to get others excited about the product and invest money in its production. You may need the services of an accountant, lawyer, banker, distributor, or vendor to make your product successful. All of these people need to buy into your idea or product. In short, you need not only a good idea, but also the ability to communicate your vision, a great business plan, and the ability to produce and sell the product with the help of your backers.

 "It's much easier to come up with ideas than to implement them."

• *Myth 5: "After a few years, I'll make lots of money."* Unless you are lucky or backed by venture capital, you probably won't get rich quick. It takes three to five years to build a profitable, viable business. If you leave a corporate job to start your own business, this is a rule of thumb for income:

  • In the first year of business, you may only make approximately 20 percent of your most recent salary.

  • By years three to five, your profits can begin to grow substantially.

You might be asking yourself, "If consultants make $1,000 to $3,000 a day, how can they not make a lot of money?" The answer is that most consultants bill for only about 55 percent of their time. The other 45 percent they spend on nonbillable activities, such as accounting, marketing, planning, and dealing with what I call "administrivia"—everything else it takes to run a business. In your first year of business, you will spend a much higher percentage of your time on nonbillable activities, such as marketing your business so that people know you exist.

If you're going to launch a business, it's best to have a dose of reality. Do your research and weigh all the factors carefully so that you can make an informed decision. Then, if the positives outweigh the negatives, by all means go for it!

Take the Entrepreneur Quiz!

HAVE YOU BEEN DOWNSIZED? Are you thinking about a career change? Are you taking early retirement? Have you said to yourself many times that you would start your own business if you only had a marketable idea? In the current economy, this may just be the time to develop a product or service and take the plunge into self-employment. Even if you have never thought of yourself as an entrepreneur, you may already have the characteristics needed to become one. And even if you don't, you can develop them—if you are willing to take on the risks involved in being an entrepreneur as well as being motivated by the rewards. The questions that follow will help you determine whether you are ready to take the plunge into business ownership.

1. Are you comfortable with NOT receiving a regular paycheck?	YES	NO
2. Do you like work that offers challenge, change, and variety, even if it involves some risk?	YES	NO
3. Are you flexible enough to meet changing market demands?	YES	NO
4. Are you willing to invest your own money as well as ask others to invest in your business venture?	YES	NO
5. Are you committed to spending as much time and effort as it takes to make your business successful?	YES	NO
6. Is it important to you to do the strategic planning as well as take care of the day-to-day details of running a business?	YES	NO

7. Is your business idea based on your expertise, interests, and solid market research?	YES NO
8. Are you able to bounce back and learn from failures or temporary setbacks?	YES NO
9. Are you optimistic, persistent, and passionate about your work?	YES NO
10. Are you confident that you are capable of succeeding as an entrepreneur?	YES NO

Scoring the Quiz

8 to 10 Yeses: *Ready to Move Ahead.* If you answered *Yes* to 8 to 10 questions, you're ready to move into starting your own business. You are willing and able to take calculated risks supported by solid information and based on experience. You are probably energized by the work you do because it's stimulating and innovative and offers you opportunities to master challenges. You are an independent thinker who is willing to listen to the advice of others but you prefer to make your own decisions. However, don't launch too fast. Be sure to write your business plan, including a marketing plan and best-case/worst-case financials. Poor planning is still one of the most common reasons for business failure.

5 to 7 Yeses: *Move Ahead Slowly.* If you answered "Yes" to 5–7 questions, you have some of the key entrepreneurial characteristics, but you need to move ahead slowly. Assess your strengths and weaknesses, and determine what you need to develop before you start a business. You might consider buying a franchise or an existing business instead of starting a business from scratch. You might also test your mettle by starting your business part-time while working for someone else full- or part-time. Grow your business slowly, and only give up your employment when it grows large enough to be a viable business.

0 to 4 Yeses: *Consider Working for Someone Else.* If you answered "Yes" to 4 or fewer of the questions, it's likely that you would be more comfortable working for someone else. You're not sure of your ability to be your own boss and do what it takes to run a business. Perhaps you are interested in starting a business because you love delivering the service or making the product. If so, you might consider working for a company that values and fosters the entrepreneurial spirit, or join a start-up team within a larger company. However, if you really want to start your own business, your determination can compensate for not having all of the entrepreneurial characteristics.

And of course, if you have a solid business idea, have evaluated the financial prospects carefully, have business partners you trust, and lots of capital, you might want to go for it.

Three Fear-Busters

No matter how you scored on this business "readiness" checklist, here are three things to keep in mind to help you get beyond the fear of taking the plunge into starting your own business:

1. You don't have to start immediately. It takes time to plan, and once you start your business it takes time to build it up. On average it takes between three and five years to build a solid, successful, profitable business. Make a plan, set your goals, and take one step at a time.

2. Marketing and selling your product or service is much easier if you believe in yourself. Base your business on your interests, strongest skills, and expertise.

3. You don't need to do it all alone. Get support from friends and family, advice from business professionals, business coaches, colleagues and take advantage of community resources. Don't fall into the trap of being the "lone wolf." This is a common mistake new entrepreneurs make. Ask for help when you need it—in the long run, you will save time and money!

CHAPTER 2

READY, SET, GO!

The Entrepreneurial Mystique

THERE'S A MYSTIQUE about the word "entrepreneur." People tend to say, "I'm not an entrepreneur. I'm a downsized executive who has a small consulting practice," or "I'm an independent contractor." I ask, "What's the difference?" Part of the mystique is thinking that the only real kind of entrepreneur is a person who has a brilliant idea and starts a business using venture capital, and the fledging enterprise becomes the next Microsoft.

Not true. According to the *Random House Dictionary*, an entrepreneur is *someone who organizes, manages, and assumes risk for a business or other enterprise.* In other words, an entrepreneur is—or can be—you.

Of course, some entrepreneurial ventures are more financially risky than others. If you are thinking about starting a business, you need to assess your level of comfort with risk, both financial and personal. Most people would try out their business schemes at least once if money were no object. However, it takes more than money to keep your venture growing and healthy. You need a passion for what you're doing, a persistent drive, and the confidence to keep up with marketplace trends.

> 4 *"If you are thinking about starting a business, you need to assess your level of comfort with risk, both financial and personal."*

What Type of Entrepreneurial Option Fits You Best?

The kind of entrepreneurial option you choose will have an effect on the risks you are willing to take. To determine what type of entrepreneurial option is best for you, assess your business vision versus how much risk you are willing

to take. Choosing your own business fit is one of the most creative and difficult aspects of going solo. In addition to thinking about whether your idea is
marketable, consider what type of work reflects your passion and promises
personal and professional fulfillment. Such a business will thrive because of
your enthusiasm and commitment.

Here are two common approaches to becoming a business owner:

1. You want to be your own boss, but you don't have a clear idea of what
   business to start.

2. You want to start a business based on your expertise, but you're afraid
   of the financial risk.

However, if your business fits your unique skills, talents, and interests,
and you have a solid plan, you can be successful either way.

Approach 1.   You want to be your own boss, but don't know what business
to start. Andrea was ready for a major life/work change. Knowing only that
she wanted to be her own boss and live in the country, she quit her corporate
job and moved to a small town in Northern California. Her business idea grew
out of her frustration with being unable to find a good pair of shoes at local
stores. She decided to fill the market void by opening a women's shoe store.

Although Andrea had no prior retail experience, she did have a background in corporate sales and marketing. She combined this savvy with the
need for stylish women's shoes at affordable prices. After three years, her store
was so successful that she sold it and opened a new store in another small
town closer to her home in the country. Andrea did not start with a brand-new
idea, but she did fill a market need that fit her skills and interests.

Approach 2.   You want to start a business based on your expertise, but
you're afraid of the financial risk. Carol was a single mom and a talented illus-
trator and graphic designer. She always wanted to be an artist, and had
worked in the graphic design field for corporations and agencies since college. Over the years, Carol managed to do freelance projects after work and
on weekends. But she was afraid to freelance full-time, because she felt she
needed to be very confident that her income would be the same (or increase)
after going solo.

However, her freelance projects began multiplying to the point where she
had no time to be with her family. After a year of almost around-the-clock
work on the job and freelance projects on top of that, she went solo. It was
a difficult and scary decision for her. Yet after one year on her own, Carol had
more work than her old job and part-time freelance work had provided com-

bined. And she loved working at home and creating designs that conveyed her customers' message colorfully, artistically, and effectively. What worked for Carol was careful planning and slowly building up a customer base in a field in which she already had expertise and contacts.

You Can Do It, Too

Both Carol and Andrea created successful businesses, even though sometimes they were scared and some of their friends thought they were crazy. You can do it, too. There are many resources and consultants to help you choose a good business fit. Surf the Internet, contact your local Chamber of Commerce or Small Business Administration, or browse through the small-business section of your local bookstore for ideas.

There is myriad information, from A to Z, detailing how to start a small business. Start planning, set goals, create your time line, and pick a starting date. Even the most confident entrepreneurs ask for help when they need it. My clients come to me, not just for a plan, but also for encouragement and to help keep them on track, maintain their focus, and build their business. That's why coaching is often part of a smart entrepreneur's plan—it gives perspective. An experienced third party can see your situation more clearly than you can, and is able to offer useful guidance and encouragement on that basis.

Taking the Leap

AS WE DISCUSSED, the *Random House Dictionary* defines an entrepreneur as "one who . . . assumes the *risk* of a business venture."

An essential element of entrepreneurship is taking calculated risks—not only when you start your business, but continually, as your business grows. Taking a calculated risk involves considering your options, knowing your business, and being ready to alter your direction when the market changes.

Christopher Brown, a successful real estate entrepreneur says, "I don't see it as a risk. Once I've made up my mind to go for it, I have enough self-confidence and follow-through to make my project fly. From my point of view, there is little risk involved." This view may sound unusual, but it doesn't have to be. If you are prepared with inner and outer resources, you stand a good chance of being able to say much the same thing to yourself some day.

Here are some of the essential inner qualities you need to take the leap:

- *Vision.* It is critical that you are able to envision your business, from start-up all the way to exit strategy. You need to know clearly what business you want to build, even if you don't know yet how you're going to do it! This also includes how your personal passion fits your business idea. Vision is the foundation from which everything is constructed in your business. Ask yourself one question: Why are you going into this business?

- *Drive.* You must be internally driven to make your vision a reality. When the going gets tough—and it will—it is dedication to your vision, along with self-motivation, that will keep you working hard to make your business profitable. It is drive—setting and achieving your goals—that propels you forward daily.

- *Confidence.* Unshakable self-confidence is crucial for building your business, no matter what circumstances arise. Authentic confidence makes people respond positively, including your customers, your employees, even your competitors. Ask yourself one question: Do you have the nerve to walk into a room full of strangers and sell them on your service?

- *Decisiveness.* Anyone can make a decision, but as an entrepreneur you have to make smart decisions based on your best attempt to gather information. You don't have time to wait for all the facts to come in before you decide. You must develop possible solutions and begin implementing them. Then, if one doesn't work, you go on to the next. Does this sound like you?

- *Flexibility.* This involves a combination of originality, curiosity, and analysis. You need to be a good troubleshooter, generate many ideas, and be open to learning about and gaining expertise in areas related to your field. You must be prepared to change plans quickly, even give up your pet ideas, in order to work efficiently and produce the results you want.

- *Powerful Communication.* When communicating with customers, clients, colleagues, or vendors, ask yourself, "What do I want specifically from this conversation? How can I communicate this clearly? What does the other person want, specifically?" Then listen carefully to their answer. As a business owner, you must be sensitive to others' expectations, needs, and signals, and be able to see things from their perspective—be able to "walk a mile in their shoes."

- *Results Orientation.* Getting things done is the lifeblood of every business. As a entrepreneur, you need to get things done efficiently and meet your deadlines on time. This takes careful planning, prioritizing your projects, following through, and solving problems on the spot.

* *Multitasking.* This means wearing many hats. If there is no one to do something, you learn how or find help. It is essential to be willing to try new things, to listen to opposing ideas, and to be a quick study. If you only want to do a certain part of the business, perhaps you should think twice about starting your own. You must be willing to do many different tasks— even those you don't like! Does this sound like you?

* *Optimistic Attitude.* High expectations equal success. Most entrepreneurs are highly motivated to succeed. They know that everything they do that is worth doing has obstacles and setbacks, just like life, and that when they experience the two-steps-forward, one-step-back syndrome, it's important to be patient enough to wait for results. It's a well-known fact that many very successful entrepreneurs had at least one failed business beforehand. Optimism also means that when you do fail, you recognize that *you* are not a failure, but it is the strategy, product, or technique that failed. You also recognize that there's most likely a better solution, which you then proceed to find. Optimists often express gratitude for what they have rather than fretting about what they don't have.

Here are thoughts about traits from some successful entrepreneurs:

"Step out and believe it's going to happen but at the same time keep your fingers crossed."
    —**Barbara Llewellyn,** Catering & Special Events

"Treat people with respect. Your job is to provide a service that helps them control the outcome of their issue or problem."
    —**Cindy Elwell,** Divorce with Dignity

"Be unwilling to fail and willing to have a mentor or two. They help you see what you can't."
    —**Heidi Paul,** WineCountry.com

"You've got to have both a head and the heart for business. The Head is how you persevere and solve problems you didn't know you could. The Heart is what shows through to the customers."
    —**Cheryl Thompson,** Bodacious Women's Club

"Stay in integrity and keep your eye on the long-term, wide view. It's the Law of Circulation: Whatever you put out there is what comes back to you."
    —**Hugh Groman,** Catering

5   *"Some entrepreneurial traits will fit you like a glove, while others will be a stretch—but all can be developed."*

Happily, you don't have to excel in all these traits. Some entrepreneurial traits will fit you like a glove, while others will be a stretch—but all can be developed, even if you are an accidental entrepreneur. Contrary to popular opinion, entrepreneurs are not born. If you study the lives of successful business owners, you will discover that one additional trait is their willingness to continually learn, develop themselves, and gain insight from their mistakes.

Ten Traits of the Successful Entrepreneur

SUCCESSFUL ENTREPRENEURS tend to share the following ten traits:

A Successful Entrepreneur:

1. Is a risk taker
2. Has a business and personal vision
3. Has drive and determination
4. Is self-confident
5. Is flexible
6. Is a powerful communicator
7. Is a smart decision maker
8. Is action/results oriented
9. Is a multitasker
10. Has an optimistic attitude

6   *"If you have a passion for doing things your way, and you have a marketable idea, you can find satisfaction and success as an entrepreneur."*

Do you think you have these traits? If so, go for it! If not, these traits can be developed. If you have a passion for doing things your way, and you have a marketable idea, you can find satisfaction and success as an entrepreneur.

Review the Ten Traits of the Successful Entrepreneur and ask yourself, "Which traits do I possess?" Write these traits inside the circle (Comfort Zone) in Figure 2-1.

Figure 2-1 Comfort Zone

Now ask yourself, "Which traits challenge me?" and write those traits outside the Comfort Zone.

Next, list a variety of ways to develop or improve those traits that are outside of your comfort zone. Talk to at least one other person to brainstorm possibilities.

Trait	How to Develop/Improve Entrepreneurial Traits

Know Why You're Going into Business

MOST LIKELY, you have taken a hard look at yourself and your finances, and you think you have what it takes to start your own business. But before you get down to the nuts and bolts of making your business a reality, ask yourself one more personal question: "What is my primary reason for starting a business?"

It is common knowledge that the first three to five years of business are critical. About half the businesses that are started fail within that time. The two factors that are mentioned most often to explain business failure are weak capitalization and poor planning. Yet when I look at successful businesses, a third reason for the failure of a business becomes clear: The business owners had weak underlying reasons for going into business. Having strong and meaningful reasons for going into business cements your commitment to a new enterprise and keeps the business going in good and bad times.

7 *"Having strong and meaningful reasons for going into business cements your commitment to a new enterprise and keeps the business going in good and bad times."*

Different Motivations of Men and Women

Different people have widely varying reasons for going into business for themselves. Men and women, in particular, often have different motivations. Research done for the Strong Interest Inventory, a career assessment tool, suggests that men and women differ not only as to why they own a business, but also in the kind of business they choose, and in their managerial style, as well. So when you are researching your business idea or getting advice, it helps to seek out people of your own sex who already own similar businesses.

The Strong Interest Inventory measures people's interests—not their abilities or skills—by comparing their results to the results of samples of people employed in more than 100 occupations who are satisfied with their careers. One occupation that is included is small business owners. The inventory's sample of small business owners includes such diverse businesses as professional services, consulting, retail sales, real estate, insurance, and skilled trades. The business structures include sole proprietors as well as fast-growing small companies. In the inventory, women entrepreneurs often said that they like to work in business settings where they can organize and structure tasks or data for well-defined projects. They are results-oriented and enjoy taking charge of the practical details necessary to solve a problem quickly and efficiently. Most often, they say that they like the specific activities of running a business and want to use their best talents. In my experience, women choose their own business more often than men do because they want to have flexible hours and make a significant contribution. They also are more likely to establish management practices, such as team management, employee autonomy, and support for work/life balance.

Men, on the other hand, prefer action-oriented environments, where they can work directly to produce tangible products or services and can work alone rather than supervise others. They are willing to work long hours, and most often they say that they want to earn a good income and like the specific activities of running a business. Men often thrive on the problem-solving aspect of running a business as well as focusing on quality control. Also, some men prefer to lead by example rather than by facilitative management.

People of both sexes tend to be enterprising types, which means they are motivated to persuade, sell, manage, and lead—all of which are important skills when starting and running a small business.

Common Reasons for Going into Business

Interests often influence the primary reason why a person chooses to run her or his own business. Common reasons include:

- Being your own boss

- Earning a good income

- Using your best skills

- Seeing the results of your work

- Having flexible hours

- Experiencing the variety of day-to-day management and tasks

- Working at home

- Developing a business around one of your strong interests

What's *your* reason? Be honest with yourself. If your primary reason is your reaction to a current workplace issue—for example, a personality conflict with your boss, a long commute, or a low salary—it may not be enough to keep you moving through the ups and downs of starting and running a business.

Cultivate Your Other Interests.   Adding to your expertise in your field makes perfect sense; however, you may think you're just too busy running a business to garden, bike, travel, or join a social club. Why pursue these interests? Because you enjoy them. Doing things you like also makes sound business sense. If you have a wide range of interests and activities, you are more interesting to others, and you can talk about a variety of topics with people you meet. In addition, you often get the best ideas in the most unlikely places—for example, you may get a solution to a nagging business problem just as you're teeing off at the 9th hole. Also, when people get to know you outside the business world, they feel comfortable referring business to you.

Your personality, expertise, enthusiasm, and financing are all very important for success. However, why you want to go into business for yourself must be compelling enough to keep you committed.

Tune Up Your Entrepreneurial Skills

THERE ARE SPECIAL TIMES in life when we remember exactly where we were, what we were doing, and how we felt—sometimes, right down to the exact minute. Was this true for you when you decided to start your own business? What excited you about taking the leap? How often have you looked back on that moment and reassessed how far you've come—what went well and what needs improvement?

8 *"Regularly reassessing your skills is as important as tuning up your car."*

Regularly reassessing your skills is as important as tuning up your car. When you tune up your car regularly, change the oil, and put air in the tires, the car runs pretty well. How about tuning up your entrepreneurial skills on a regular basis? Work requires three types of skills:

1. Personal traits

2. Transferable skills

3. Expertise specific to your industry or business

Chances are that you build on your expertise daily, in the course of doing your business. Now could be a good time to reflect on your personal traits to decide which traits need some improvement, so that you'll be even more successful in your business.

Personal Trait Tune-Up Assessment

Here are some entrepreneurial traits that may need tuning up:

- *Drive.* You must be internally driven—self-motivated. A plan without commitment gets you nowhere. When the going gets tough (and it will), try to rekindle that initial spark that made you want to start a business in the first place. It's dedication to your vision and determination that will keep you working hard to make your business a success.

- *Self-Confidence.* This is the one trait that is difficult to maintain, especially when business is taking a downturn. You need unmistakable confidence in yourself and belief in your product or service. Entrepreneurs are optimistic: They know they can master challenges, bounce back from defeat, and realize goals. They may have strong egos, but they are not self-important. Even the most confident entrepreneurs ask for feedback to assess how well they are doing.

- *Adaptability.* This may well be the "mantra" of the modern workplace. You need to be a good troubleshooter, to generate many new ideas, and to be open to learning about and gaining expertise in related areas. Stay flexible—prepare to change plans quickly, even to give up your most cherished ideas, in order to work efficiently and produce the results you want. It's important to be honest, realistic, and confront mistakes, and then take steps to find workable solutions.

- *Communication.* Effective communication is essential. When communicating with your customers, clients, and colleagues, you must ask for what you want, clearly and specifically. As a business owner or consultant, you must listen first in order to be sensitive to others' expectations, needs, and signals, and then figure out how to respond for maximum effect. For example, if a customer is complaining about service, you might try listening to what that person is really saying, and then work together to find a solution. If you are going to be an effective communicator, you need to empathize with others' needs and see things from their perspective—to "walk a mile in their shoes."

Taking Steps Toward Your Own Personal Tune-Up

Try the following steps for your personal tune-up:

Tune In. Focus on those traits you considered in the beginning, when you first asked yourself, "Do I have what it takes to start my own business?"

- What traits did you identify? _____
- Which traits need some improvement? _____

Diagnosis. Determine your strengths and weaknesses. Pick two skills that are not up to the level you need (where you feel the current level holds you back in your business). Those are the ones that can use a tune-up.

Skill #1: _____

Skill #2: _____

Create a Tune-Up Plan. Figure out what aspect of your business needs to be tweaked to improve it. Find a mentor or coach who has years of experience in business. Ask customers, colleagues, and professional contacts. Create a plan and build a support system to keep you on track.

Consider doing this tune-up every six months—for example, in January and June. Set goals. Make sure your goals are SMART goals: **S**pecific, **M**easurable, **A**ctionable, **R**ealistic, and within a **T**imeframe. For example: "By May 30, schedule four talks at local professional organizations, and then deliver these talks by August 1." Just as your car's fuel light comes on to remind you to get gas, build in a reminder to upgrade your entrepreneurial skills on a regular basis.

Avoid the Seven Common Pitfalls in Business

ACCORDING TO THE Small Business Administration, "50 percent of new businesses in the United States fail within the first four years. Those 20 percent that survive in business ten years or more learn to leverage existing skills and utilize experts to help their businesses."

9 *"Both newly minted and experienced entrepreneurs discover that building and marketing their business takes longer than they thought."*

Why? There are so many pitfalls to trip over, but that doesn't stop people from trying—like you. Both newly minted and experienced entrepreneurs discover that building and marketing their business takes longer than they thought.

In this chapter, I share with you what it takes to be successful—how to strengthen your entrepreneurial muscles—and how to avoid the most common pitfalls in business.

Going solo is challenging. Many entrepreneurs jump in with no planning and end up spending money unwisely, wasting valuable time, and resources. At least knowing about and preparing for the following seven pitfalls helps companies prepare for the new path they're taking. Building your business is creating the business you've always dreamed about. Why not set goals for your dream and work toward a deadline? By avoiding the 7 common pitfalls you will be able to reach your goals one step at a time by helping you to:

- Choose marketing strategies wisely while saving time and money.

- Get more clients and earn more money by using time more effectively.

- Manage the hardships along the way, create a marketing plan, and give yourself benchmarks to help you stay on track.

Pitfall 1: If You Can't Describe It You Can't Sell It!

Clear communication is the key. When you describe your business or introduce yourself, it is essential that people understand and know what you sell. That's why one essential communication tool is your 30-second elevator speech that needs to clearly convey what you offer clients.

Here is an example of an elevator speech that does not clearly communicate what the business offers:

We work with any company's staff members who are responsible for both the efficient use of the company's interior space and facilitating the ongoing relocation of their employees; a staff increasingly struggling with balancing the constant upsizing and downsizing challenges of their company with fewer in-house staff to make it happen.

We help solve the problem of supplementing your in-house staff with an experienced technical know-how, proven team communication skills, and rapid, reliable responsiveness to the inevitable changes that occur during the life of your project.

Here is a simplified version:

Our company _____ (name) is an expert at helping companies plan and implement a move. We take care of all equipment, electronics, furniture, phones, computers, and even delicate scientific instruments to ensure you'll have everything working once your move is completed—on time and on budget.

Which introduction do you think is more successful in making a sale?

Key to remember: Make it simple and easy for customers to understand what you are selling and how it solves their problems.

Pitfall 2: Don't Leap Before You Know What It Takes to Succeed

There are four essential ingredients to creating, building, and maintaining a thriving business. Be prepared by knowing these key factors that influence business success even during tough economic times.

The First Key Success Factor: Confidence.   You need unmistakable confidence in yourself and belief in your product or service. Entrepreneurs are optimistic; they know they can master challenges, bounce back from defeat, and realize goals. This is the one trait that is difficult to maintain especially when business is taking a downturn. Even the most confident entrepreneurs ask for feedback to assess how well they are doing. That's why many entrepreneurs work with business consultants, coaches, or mentors to get expert advice, perspective, and encouragement. Imagine that you have a confidence barometer on your refrigerator. Each morning, ask: How am I doing today? Then, plan your day accordingly.

The Second Key Success Factor: Connections.   Establish connections with professional or trade associations in your field for contacts, referrals, and support. Build community. Be visible. Be generous. Build and nurture your personal network. Relationships are the building blocks of business.

The Third Key Success Factor: Competence.   Expertise. Quality. Make it easy to do business with you. A well-developed product, delivered on time with excellent customer service, is a winning combination. When you're starting out, ask: How do I market myself? If you have years of experience in the field, you are an expert.

A *sub-pitfall* is: Even if you're an expert you still need to be able to sell your expertise. So you may need to develop your competence in selling. Some of the best experts—like lawyers, physicians, and MBAs—need to learn how to market themselves.

**TIPS TO BOOST YOUR CONFIDENCE AND
COMPETENCE AT THE BEGINNING**

- Take classes to develop your competency level.

- Find a mentor who is an expert in your profession or field or an expert in marketing and sales.

The Fourth Key Success Factor: Capital.   It's hard to be creative when you're worried about your mortgage. Unless your business is a candidate for venture capital, you, your family, and friends will finance your business. Have a minimum of six to twelve months of living expenses to start. Remember that it takes three to five years to build a profitable business. And remember also to use your own money: You'll spend it more wisely.

In summary, answer these questions for yourself:

* What is your confidence level?

* Are you well connected? Do you have an active professional network?

* In what areas do you feel competent and what do you need to develop?

* How will you finance your business and keep your doors open in those first two crucial years?

When you've answered these questions to your own satisfaction, you will know when you're ready to take the leap—because you will have analyzed your situation and developed an initial plan. Careful planning pays off. Use your time, talent, and resources to the best advantage.

Pitfall 3: Don't Be a Lone Wolf

Many business owners fail because they don't ask for the help they need.

What does it take to succeed? To succeed you need to be able to ask for help in order to move forward, to monitor your growth process, and to have advice at critical stages of your business. For example, ask for help when you are ready to sign a large contract, to hire new employees, or to gain new knowledge, tips, and resources to keep on track with your goals.

TIPS

* Did you know that creating your business idea and then actually making it happen reside in two different parts of your brain? Because there is a dichotomy between your creative and practical abilities, you can undermine yourself at every turn. Learn how to delegate tasks that you are not good at or that can be done by a part-time administrative assistant.

* It's hard to do it all yourself, which is where many entrepreneurs go wrong. Get help when you need it. It is scary to be all alone and responsible for every part of your business. The self-made man is a myth!

> • You wear many hats as a solo entrepreneur. You are the CEO, CFO, COO, CIO, VP of Marketing and Sales, and chief cook and bottle washer. Plan for growth early. Decide when to hire your first employee (which often may be an administrative assistant), or obtain a business partner so that you can pass off some of your hats and focus on what you do best.

Help and resources are available in person with consultants and coaches, and your local SBA office. They can help you avoid taking on full-time staff, while offering their experience and guidance that is personalized to your issues and business. You can also get some information online, in books, classes, workshops, and from state and local governmental agencies and chambers of commerce.

Pitfall 4: Jumping the Gun without Market Research and Planning

A majority of new business owners open their doors with little market research and planning. Just doing it can work, but will probably cost you more time, sometimes several years, and loss of some of your investment capital. However, a marketing plan gives you direction and benchmarks, and it can save you time and money.

To avoid this pitfall, this is how you can put smart and planful marketing into effect.

Ingredients of Smart and Planful Marketing

• Define your business products or services clearly

• Define your market specifically

• Conduct market research and know your competition

• Define your positioning, that which makes you unique

The following example can serve as a model of how to revamp your positioning: A human resource consulting firm that provides personnel hiring and retention services for small businesses asked us to help define their niche market so they'd know who best to go after to find more clients to grow their firm.

As a first step, we defined their market as small to medium businesses with gross revenues around $5 to 20 million, without an in-house human resources staff, and not yet under contract with another human resources firm. As a second step, we conducted competitive market research to find out what others are offering like they do, what area they might be missing or which audience might not be served. We found that there were literally hundreds of competitors with varying degrees of talent and difficulty in working with them.

Lastly, we determined positioning by establishing how they were perceived by their current clients compared to their competitors. We found, for example, that their actual human resource services weren't considered very special at all, but clients simply loved this company. Why do you suppose? It turns out they were delightful to work with, easy to get along with, and they delivered quality services while still being flexible with the particular needs of their clients.

As a result, we determined their positioning as professional and skillful, but more importantly, as really nice to work with. This enabled them to rewrite their marketing materials and in-person presentations to reflect this finding. People understood who they were and what they were good at.

Pitfall 5: One Size Doesn't Fit All When Marketing Your Business

It is essential to create a comprehensive and integrated marketing plan tailor-made for your business. Here are some tips to help you do that:

Tip 1.   Don't pick the easiest, cheapest tool or just the ones you already know how to do—it may not be best for your business. This is a marketing pitfall that catches so many new businesses. Even if you don't feel comfortable with a particular marketing technique, it may be just the right one for your type of business.

An example is an estate planner who hates public speaking but knows that seminars work well for marketing her services. It is important for her to figure out how to integrate seminars into her marketing plan because they give her the opportunity to outreach to a large number of prospective clients and tell them what estate planning is all about and how she can help them. One solution might be teaming up with a financial planner and presenting together.

Tip 2.   Sometimes you need to just do it or to test ideas to really find out whether they work for your business. Don't get stuck in analysis paralysis but start by:

- Testing your sales pitch or ideas on friends or colleagues (or professionals if you can afford them). Ask them if they'd buy your service and what they'd pay.

- Ask them to repeat back to you what it is they'd buy so you can see if people really understand your product or service.

Tip 3.   Make sure you diversify your marketing portfolio. Choose from the tips in many areas so you reach as much of your target market in as many ways through as many types of media as you can.

To start out, use a combination of media: ads, a website, direct mail, publicity, and networking. Why do this? To reach as much of your target market as possible in as many ways as you can. Keep in mind that not everyone reads magazines, goes to your website, reads your e-mail, reads your articles online, or meets you at networking events.

Tip 4.   Last, don't sacrifice sales while doing your marketing. Marketing just supports sales.

- If you think of sales as building relationships or solving other people's problems, suddenly you've taken that negative connotation out of it.

- Small business is about building relationships, understanding what people want, and making sure you or your product are a good fit for their needs.

- It is important to listen to what your market wants from you, what they will pay, and what they want changed about your product or service in order to buy it.

- Remember, people refer to and buy from whom they know and trust.

Pitfall 6: If You Can't Visualize It, You Can't Make It Happen

To help you apply all you've learned and researched about your business so far and bring your new business or new idea into reality, here is a simple tool to use. The key is to clearly visualize what you want for your business because then you can make it happen.

If you have already been in business for several years, what are some of the projects, products, or expansion ideas that you might want to consider in the future? Try this exercise:

Visualization

1. What are you selling?

2. Whom are you helping?

3. Who is helping you sell or make your product or provide service?

4. What resources do you have now that you can use in your business (e.g., computer, phone, home office, credit line, or financial investor)?

5. How are you financing your business?

6. How does business success look to you?

In the spaces above, write down just the key kernels of wisdom you elicited from doing this visualization. This now can become the purpose or vision section of your business and/or marketing plan to bring your vision to fruition.

Pitfall 7: No Built-In Focus and Accountability

Have someone you are accountable to. This will help you stay on track, keep your focus, and build your business. Often, coaching or mentoring is part of their plan. Why? Accountability and encouragement make it all happen. What does a coach or mentor offer?

1. *Perspective.* An experienced third party can see more clearly than you and offer useful guidance. They help you get unstuck as well as assist you in facing important issues so that you can move forward. They give you a boost when you're down or feeling overwhelmed.

2. *Experience.* Work with people who know your business well or who have been in business so that they can help you plan for the expected and unexpected. They offer support, consultation, and strategies and tools that make sense as your business grows.

3. *Accountability*. Third parties can help you accelerate growth faster than you could yourself. They can help you track your results so you can measure what is and what is not working. Track marketing as well as finances. The predominant mistake people make in marketing is not reviewing their marketing results. Third parties might also help you set up a database, spreadsheets, or whatever works for you. In the first two years, you want to know that you can meet your financial obligations and keep your business running even if you are not making a profit yet.

When you're starting out, interview professionals in your industry. Find out how they started and how they overcame obstacles along the way. I stumbled along and figured things out as I went. I finally discovered that hiring professionals got me where I wanted to go faster. My business coach helped me develop my leadership skills.

—**Barbara Llewellyn,** Barbara Llewellyn Catering & Event Planning, Oakland, California

Now that you know the seven common pitfalls and ways to avoid them, you're ready to go out there and build a fantastically successful business. Remember:

- Communicate clearly.

- Leap when you're ready.

- Don't be a lone wolf.

- Use the smart and planful approach to marketing.

- Create a comprehensive marketing plan that fits your business.

- Visualize what you want your business to be.

- Keep your focus and stay accountable to your plan.

CHAPTER 3

TAKING CARE OF BUSINESS

A Name That Grows with Your Business

"**WHAT'S IN A NAME?**" A great deal when it comes to the word or phrase that characterizes and brands your business. Naming your business is both exciting and difficult. The name you choose for your business creates the image of your company. Always think about how your business will be perceived by others—customers, vendors, competitors, and the rest of the business community. You want to be taken seriously in the marketplace. How do you name your business? If you have developed your own business, the choice is yours. You want to choose a name that reflects both the essence of your business and you. If you have purchased a franchise, the decision has already been made for you. And if you have bought an existing business, you may decide to change its name. However, research this carefully so that you don't lose market share because of a name change.

10 "Always think about how your business will be perceived by others—customers, vendors, competitors, and the rest of the business community."

No matter what type of business you're naming, consider these four points:

1. *Make sure the name fits your business.* You want customers to clearly understand what product or service you offer. For example, "JRG Associates" might indicate that the business involves consultants, but does not reveal what type of consulting the company offers. "Don

Hayne's Automotive Shop," on the other hand, clearly says what the company does.

2. *Make sure that the company name is easy to pronounce, spell, and remember.*

3. *Make sure that the name allows for the growth of your business.* Five years into your business, you may decide to expand by adding new products and services. Make sure that your name is flexible enough to include the new additions. For example, if you start by selling candy under the name "Candy Corner," most of your products will need to be related to candy. However, if you name the business "Sweet Treats," you have many options about what to sell in your store.

4. *Research the names you are considering to make sure they are available.* Check to make sure that the name has not been previously filed in your city or county as a fictitious name, or nationally trademarked (^{TM}), service marked (SM), or registered (®).

Before you actually make the crucial decision of a name, consider these questions:

• Is your business local? If your business is local and does not contain your own name as all or part of it, file a fictitious name (also known as a DBA—"Doing business as . . .") in your city and county. This means that no one else in your city and county should be able to use the same or similar name, usually for a period of five years.

• Is your own name part of your business name, as in "Peter Smith Print Shop"? If so, you don't need to worry about registering a fictitious name or a trademark because the name can only be yours. However, to be on the safe side, do a search before registering to be sure there isn't another Peter Smith Print Shop in the county.

• Do you want a logo to be an integral part of your business name? Do you want to do business nationally? If your answer is yes to one or both of these questions, you may need to consider trademarking or service marking your name and logo. A trademark (^{TM}) is defined as "either a word, phrase, symbol, or design, or combination of words, phrases, symbols or designs, which identifies and distinguishes the source of the goods or services of one party from those of others." A service mark (SM) is the same as a trademark except that it identifies and distinguishes the source of a service.

Remember that your fictitious name is only yours in your own city or county. Someone else can file the same name in a different county or state. The main reason to consider a trademark is to protect your name and your product/service. Also, you've probably spent a lot of time, effort, and perhaps money choosing the name and logo that is just right for you. It would be a shame for someone else to choose the same name and trademark it. It is very expensive to have to redo all of your promotional collateral and advertisements, business cards, letterhead, and signage, not to mention building up name recognition for your business again. Find out more about trademarks on the web by going to uspto.gov.

• Do you plan to market or sell your products/services online? Even if you don't plan to sell on the Web, many consultants advise having a presence on the Web—which means you need to have a website. It's a good idea to have as your own domain name either the actual name of your business or something close to it. Early in the naming process, make a list of prospective names and find out which of them are still available as domain names.

Remember that if your exact name is already taken as a domain name, you can add numbers or change the name in some way to make it yours. For example, "Wacky Widgets" might already be taken, but "wackywidgets123" may be available. Be creative in naming your business—but don't rush it. Take your time. That name will be associated with you for a long time.

A Checklist for Setting Up Your Business

STARTING YOUR OWN BUSINESS is exhilarating and exciting. However, there is important paperwork to contend with in order to meet and implement all the legal requirements and guidelines required to establish your business. Doing your homework in the beginning will save you costly mistakes and create fewer problems after you open your business door.

For most businesses, you need to decide on your business structure, get a fictitious name (DBA, or "Doing business as . . ."), a business license, insurance, and pay self-employment taxes (approximately 15 percent of net earnings, paid quarterly) to the IRS. However, legal requirements and guidelines vary according to your type of business and location. For example, if you are manufacturing products for sale or working in the food/beverage industry, you may be required to get permits from federal, state, and local agencies. Make sure you ask an attorney as well as people in your line of business plenty of questions so you don't miss something that you need in order to "legalize" your business.

Following is the basic information that will get you started:

Ensuring Your Business Name

If you plan to conduct business under a fictitious name, you must file a "DBA" ("Doing business as . . .") unless you are a corporation, in which case your name is ensured when you incorporate. In either case, you are using a name for your business that is not directly recognizable as your business because your own name is not connected to it.

There are two parts to the process of filing a DBA:

1. *Filing with the County Clerk.* You must file the Fictitious Name statement with the City or County Clerk. You will receive proof from the Clerk that it has been properly recorded. Fees for this service vary between $20 and $50, and it is generally valid for four to five years.

2. *Publishing Your Fictitious Name.* Your notice of conducting business under a fictitious name must be published in a general circulation newspaper (of your choice) in the county in which your business will be located. This notice must appear in four consecutive editions. It makes sense to choose the least expensive publication in your area for this service.

Obtaining a Business License

To operate within the law, apply for a business license or permit in the city or county where your business is located. Call your city or county office to ask about local requirements. The requirements and fee structures for business licenses vary from community to community, and these licenses are taken quite seriously. The licenses provide a source of revenue for the city or county, and they are a means of regulating the types of businesses allowed to operate within their jurisdictions. A business license is proof to the IRS that you are in business. Business licenses are renewed annually, and most cities will send you a reminder in the mail.

Obtaining a Seller's Permit

If you purchase items for resale or provide a taxable service, a seller's permit is required in all states where sales tax is collected. This permit means that you can collect the required sales tax on that item/service, and you are held accountable for forwarding the collected tax to the state's Department of Revenue. As the business owner, you are liable and responsible for paying the sales tax. In California, the State Board of Equalization is responsible for issuing seller's permits. For detailed information, contact your regional State Board of Equalization.

Obtaining Insurance

Depending on the nature and complexity of your business, you may need a variety of insurance policies to protect you, your assets, and your customers. Think of insurance as an investment in your business. Get further information from your insurance agent. Types of insurance to consider are:

- General liability

- Professional liability (for consultants)

- Fire

- Workers' compensation (if you have employees)

- Product liability

- Health

- Key man

- Business property

- Business interruption

Deciding on Business Structures

Which type of "legal" business structure is best for you? This is an important decision, and one that you can't easily change. The three basic structures are: sole proprietor, partnership, and corporation. Each has advantages and disadvantages. There are also several types of partnerships and corporate structures to choose from. Consult an attorney or business advisor if you are in doubt.

- *Sole proprietorship.* This structure is the easiest and least expensive to establish. You are the sole owner of profits and losses. You have total control over business decisions, and you are taxed as an individual.

- *Partnership.* In this structure, two or more people agree to share ownership and management of the business. An advantage is that it gives you access to more available resources, talents, and skills. Profits and losses are shared among the partners as agreed upon. But make sure you have a written partnership agreement. Many friendships have been lost when partnerships go bad.

- *Corporation.* This is the most expensive and regulated structure. A corporation is a distinct legal entity separate from the individuals who own it. The corporation owns assets and assumes debt separate from the owners. It has the ability to raise substantial capital for growth and expansion. You are taxed twice: You pay income tax on corporate net income (profit) *and* on your individual salary and dividends.

11 *"The more information you gather on licenses, insurance, and taxes, the less overwhelming the paperwork will be."*

The more information you gather on licenses, insurance, and taxes, the less overwhelming the paperwork will be. If you proceed step by step through the requirements discussed in this chapter, this seemingly overwhelming task will be more manageable and less stressful. Build in sufficient time to complete this part of your business plan.

Are You an Independent Contractor or an Employee?

MANY FREELANCERS and consultants choose to work as independent contractors, and love working for a variety of companies on many different projects. However, it's important to know whether you are really considered an independent contractor in the eyes of the IRS.

Independent contractors are self-employed businesspeople who are hired by a company to perform specific projects—for example, delivering training programs, or fixing software applications as a computer specialist. Independent contractors are much like vendors, except that they perform intangible services rather than supplying goods.

The general rule of thumb is that a worker at a company is not an independent contractor if the company has the right to direct the person with respect to when, where, and how the project work is to be performed. If the company specifies only the desired results of the project, the person is usually considered to be an independent contractor.

There's a lot of room for interpretation in this arrangement. Even when the company does not exert control, if it appears that the company has the right to control how a contractor completes a project, the independent contractor may be reclassified (by the IRS) as an employee. The reason the IRS is interested in reclassifying independent contractors is that an employer is required to withhold taxes from employees' pay, whereas the government depends on self-employed individuals to report their own taxable income. There are about two dozen factors the IRS looks at to decide whether or not a worker is actually an independent contractor.

> # 12
> "If it appears that the company has the right to control how a contractor completes a project, the independent contractor may be reclassified (by the IRS) as an employee."

The following is a list of the thirteen most common factors. As an independent contractor, protect yourself by making sure at the beginning of a contract that:

1. You request a thorough contract with the company, which clearly states (a) the specific results you are expected to achieve for a project, and (b) that you, as the independent contractor, determine the ways and means of completing the project.

2. You obtain specifications regarding the outcome of the project, but don't ask for instructions from management.

3. You accept no company-sponsored training program. The IRS views this as "employee" development.

4. You ask that the work duration be limited to a specific time period for one or more specific projects. Include this in a written contract.

5. You invoice the company on a project basis, even if you are doing several projects for the same company.

6. You require no set hours of work, although you can specify approximate hours per week and completion deadlines.

7. You specify your own place of work, if possible, for the particular project.

8. You pay your own expenses.

9. You do contract work for more than one company.

10. You show that you are a business by having a business name, by using your own business cards, and by being incorporated. (Note: Being a sole proprietor with a "DBA" may not be enough.)

11. You may work among the staff on-site, but not as an integral part of a company project team.

12. You voluntarily choose to provide oral or written progress reports with respect to meeting deadlines. However, the company cannot require you to submit such reports.

13. You make sure your contract agreement contains termination limitations so that the company cannot terminate you "at will," as it can with employees.

These are useful guidelines. However, they do not replace a consultation with a competent attorney or tax advisor about your specific case. You can obtain further information from your local Employee Development Department (Form # DE38: *Employment Determination Guide*), and from the Internal Revenue Service, which offers guidance in *IRS Publication 1976*. Remember, it is in the company's best interest to follow the basic guidelines for independent contractors, because there are serious tax consequences to the company for not doing so. The IRS always fines the company, not the contractor. However, it is also in your best interest to make sure you meet the qualifications as an independent contractor. The guidelines can be very confusing, so don't assume that your client company is up to speed on the regulations.

Which Business Structure Is Best for You?

AND NOW LET'S TAKE an expanded look into business structures. The following information is offered as a general overview of your choices for the "legal structure" of your business. However, when in doubt, seek the counsel of an attorney or a business advisor.

Sole Proprietorship

This is the easiest, least expensive, and most common form of business structure. A sole proprietorship is owned and operated by one person (spouses are considered as One). Sole proprietorships may have employees.

Advantages

- Easy to organize.

- You are the sole owner of the profits (and you are also responsible for the losses).

- Least expensive to establish. Costs vary according to the city in which the business is formed, but usually they include a license fee and may include a business tax. Check the requirements in your city and county.

- Less reporting. Generally, a sole proprietorship can be established by registering your company's name (filing a DBA) and obtaining a business license.

- No double tax, because you are taxed as an individual. Your business profit and loss is recorded on Federal Tax Form 1040, Schedule C, and the net profit or loss is transferred to your personal tax form. You will also file Schedule E, which is your contribution to Social Security. (Caution: This is equal to 15 percent of the net profit or loss.)

- Total control and freedom to act. The business is owned and operated by you.

Disadvantages

- Unlimited liability. You are responsible for all business debt. This liability extends to all your assets, including your home and vehicle.

- Less available capital. Funding must come from the owner, and obtaining long-term financing may be difficult. Loans are based on your individual financial strength.

- Limited growth potential. The growth of the company is dependent upon your capabilities.

- Death, illness, or injury can endanger the business. The business ceases to exist as a legal entity upon the death of the owner.

General Partnership

This is a legal and more formal business relationship in which two or more people agree to share ownership and management of a business.

Advantages

- Ease of formation. Regulations vary by state, but generally a partnership can be established by registering the company's name (filing a DBA) and obtaining a business license.

- Combination of resources and talents. Two—or more—heads are better than one! A partnership allows for distribution of the workload and for sharing of ideas, skills, and responsibilities. It also makes it possible to obtain more capital and to tap into more skills.

- Personal tax benefits.

Disadvantages

- Unlimited liability. The owners are personally responsible for the business debt. Profits must be included on each partner's individual tax return, according to their percentage of interest in the business. Further, each partner may be liable for the other's "bad business judgment." Make sure you have a written partnership agreement!

- Lack of continuity. The partnership terminates upon the death or withdrawal of a general partner, unless the partnership agreement provides otherwise. Death, withdrawal, or bankruptcy of one partner can endanger the entire business.

- Relative difficulty in obtaining large sums of capital. Long-term financing is still dependent upon review of each individual partner's assets.

- Difficulty in disposing of the partnership interest. The buying out of a partnership or sale to another party must be spelled out in the partnership agreement. Otherwise, the business will suffer while the dispute continues.

- Distribution of responsibility in bankruptcy. In case of bankruptcy, the partner with more personal assets will lose more. Be aware of this!

13 *"Select your partners carefully, because you are bound by each other's decisions!"*

- Partner's responsibility. Select your partners carefully, because you are bound by each other's decisions! Each partner represents the company and can individually hire employees, borrow money, and operate the business.

- Profits. Profits are shared among the partners according to the terms outlined in your partnership agreement.

Limited Partnership

In a general partnership, as discussed above, the partners equally share the responsibilities associated with managing and financing the business, as well as the liability. In a *limited partnership*, the partners risk only their investment; if they do not participate in the management or control of the business, they are not subject to the same liabilities as in a general partnership.

Advantages

- General partners have additional capital invested.
- Limited partners have limited liability, equal to their investment.
- Allocation of income and losses may provide tax benefits.

Disadvantages

- Limited partners have no control over the management of the business.
- Partnership profits are taxed as income to the partners.

Corporation

Although the corporation is the most complex business structure of all, it can afford peace of mind for the business principals. A corporation is a distinct legal entity, separate from the individuals who own it. It literally stands apart from the owners and is treated as an independent unit. The "corporation" owns assets and assumes debt separately from the owners.

Advantages

- Ownership is readily transferable. The corporation does not cease to exist with the death of an owner, but continues operating.
- Increased opportunities for growth and fundraising. A corporation has access to a broader range of investors and can raise substantial capital through the sale of stock.

- The corporation is a separate and legal entity. It is responsible and liable for all debts. The shareholders are liable only for the amount they have invested.

- Authority can be delegated. The corporation has the ability to draw on the expertise and skills of more than one individual.

Disadvantages

- Extensive government regulations. Corporations are complex to manage, and are highly regulated. Tedious local, state, and federal reports must be filed, and annual stockholder meetings must be held. Because of the complexity of establishing and maintaining the corporate entity, it is advisable to work with an attorney.

- High costs of forming and maintaining a corporation. The fees for setting up a corporate structure in California range from $900 to $3,000. The expenses for legal fees and paperwork are ongoing.

- Increased tax load. Income tax is paid on the corporate net income (profit) and on individual salaries and dividends. In other words, you are doubly taxed.

S Corporation

The S Corporation status allows a small business to have its income taxed to the shareholders as if the corporation were a partnership. This specifically addresses the issue of double taxation. Talk to your attorney or accountant to determine if this form of legal structure is right for your business. Specific conditions for making and maintaining an S Corporation are:

- The corporation is limited to 10 shareholders, all of which are individuals or estates.

- Only one class of stock is allowed.

- A specific portion of the corporation's receipts must be derived from active business rather than passive investments.

- No limit is placed on the size of the corporation's income and assets.

- All shareholders must consent to the election of S corporation treatment.

- The corporation must operate on a calendar year.

Limited Liability Company

The Limited Liability Company (LLC) is the newest form of business legal structure that allows owners the protection from personal liability that is provided to the corporate structure and the pass-through taxation of the partnership. Laws regarding the LLC are evolving, and some issues are complicated. Most certainly, discuss this option with an attorney and/or an accountant to determine the best course of action for your business. Here is a list of advantages and disadvantages of an LLC:

Advantages

- LLC partners have complete management and control of the business while also enjoying limited liability. However, if the number of partners exceeds 15 to 20, it is probably better to form a corporation to most efficiently manage the business.

- An LLC works well for professional service businesses, such as lawyers and commercial real estate developers and investors.

- An LLC can also work well for start-up companies because they can deduct the losses that they expect in the first few years of business.

- The additional required record keeping on management decisions can help to avoid disputes among partners.

Disadvantages

- It is better and less complicated to incorporate when the company is a capital-intensive, fast-growing start-up that plans to seek outside investment capital, to offer equity sharing plans to employees, or to do an IPO. There is ongoing record keeping required. All states require LLCs to file "Articles of Organization" and charge a filing fee. In California, the filing fee is $800 per year.

- LLCs with more than twenty partners need to hire a manager to manage the business on behalf of the larger, more inactive membership. This can get complicated and expensive.

To Partner or Not to Partner

THERE COMES A TIME in the life of your business when you need to consider a partnership as a way to meet marketplace needs, opportunities, or to expand. Here are a couple of ways to do this:

1. *Create a partnership with a competitor, a new investor, or a talented colleague whose strengths complement yours.* You join together and create one business. For example, let's say there are two hat companies in the same city. One specializes in women's hats and one in men's. The marketplace favors one-stop shopping. You provide it together, as the XYZ Hat Company. Be sure to read up on the details of partnerships in the next section and write and sign a partnership agreement. (See Chapter 13.)

2. *Create a strategic alliance.* Say that you want to build your business but can't do it on your own, or you don't want to hire employees. Or perhaps a current client has asked you to do a project, and you don't have the expertise to handle a part of it—and you don't want to say "No." Instead of taking on unwanted new employees or recruiting a permanent partner, you can team up with another consultant or business to jointly market and deliver that particular product or service. Your businesses remain separate, but you subcontract with each other to deliver the service under one business name. However, there is no *new* business entity; one business owner just subcontracts with the other owner.

After the venture is complete, you and your strategic partner may decide to continue working together on the same product/service, or to create a new project that fits both of your businesses. For example, a marketing consultant and a CPA might form a strategic alliance to offer a start-up package that includes a marketing plan, financial projections, and coaching to people who want to start a small business or grow their existing business. Of course, you and your strategic partner may also decide not to continue working together, once the initial joint project is complete.

For both ways of partnering, be sure to draw up a written contract that all parties involved agree to and sign. Once you decide to work together, the following seven principles will help ensure success and increased revenue for your business:

1. *Have an idea that's bigger than you are.* Your vision for the expansion of your business needs to be greater than just you. It's obvious that you can't accomplish it alone. All partners need a shared vision, commitment to purpose, follow through, and teamwork.

2. *Be honest about your personal goals.* Understand each other's agendas and methods for building your joint business projects. It is also essential to be straight about how much time and money you will contribute to each project and to clearly identify how you will share profits and handle losses. It needs to be a win-win situation for all involved.

3. *Keep the lines of communication open.* Include input from all partners, especially when making major decisions. In the case of strategic partnerships, it's crucial that everyone involved share clearly what each individual business culture needs. Each joint project needs a point person. This person will act as the decision maker for daily operations.

4. *Have a plan for every project.* Develop a joint business plan for each strategic project. Make sure that you lay it out carefully, measurable objective by measurable objective, step by step, with specific assignments for all involved—what I call "what by when and by whom."

5. *Do customer-focused marketing.* You need to be focused on the customer, be nimble, and constantly assess the market so that your positioning is right. This is an ongoing process. You need to take a fresh look in order to adjust your offerings to meet your customers' needs.

6. *Be alert to problem solving.* In every project, there will be bumps along the way. Do regular reality checks, revise your plans as necessary, and communicate when problems arise so you don't let misunderstandings fester. If your joint mission and commitment are great enough, good planning and communications will help you handle problems and keep on moving.

7. *Don't forget to celebrate.* When you achieve your project goals, celebrate your victory. Do something outrageous to acknowledge your hard work. Give crazy awards. Stop. Reflect. Savor.

14 *"Evaluate all aspects of the project, the partnership, and your business mission before you move on to the next phase of your business growth and partnership."*

Finally, don't forget to evaluate all aspects of the project, the partnership, and your business mission before you move on to the next phase of your business growth and partnership. Learning from the mistakes you made the first time around is essential for a dynamic, strong, and vibrant partnership.

Partnerships that Work

THERE IS MUCH WRITTEN about why partnerships fail. Some say that dissolving a business partnership is more difficult than a divorce. You have just read about the advantages and disadvantages of business partnership. In this chapter, I want to showcase how partnerships can work wonderfully well to grow vital, thriving, profitable businesses. There are a variety of challenges even in the best of partnerships, and especially with partners who are friends or family. All business owners have asked themselves at some point: How do I want to spend my day at work? Do I enjoy myself around the people I work with? How much interaction do I want with my partner and employees? Is the partnership decision strictly about the money? The answers to these questions are factors in deciding whether to have a partner and who the best-fit partner might be.

As Cheryl Thompson of the Bodacious Women's Club says, "My partner and I admire the qualities and skills in each other and celebrate strengthening each of our gifts or talents." It is a common theme that the roles and skills of each partner must complement each other and be vital to the growth of the business. Also, when things get tough, and they do, timely open and honest communication is a key ingredient to the health of the business and the emotional health of the partners.

Here are five real entrepreneurial partnership success stories:

Founder and Employee Partners

In 1983, Michael Dennison founded Bavarian Professionals, a BMW Auto Repair Shop in Berkeley, California. Ten years into business, Michael hired a young man as manager, Nate, to take over the day-to-day operations. This freed up Michael to focus on new projects and spend more time with his family. By hiring a manager, Michael achieved his definition of success: to run his business profitably without the day-to-day oversight of the owner. Michael says, "Reaching this goal can be very elusive. The person who replaces the founder must be well compensated so that he is motivated and driven to succeed as well."

Partnership Roles

Michael's payoff is to continue to generate robust, steady income and, as the founding partner, to do so by working just twenty hours a week. After eleven years he made the operations manager a 50 percent partner in the business. Why? "Nate is an integral part of the team, has been instrumental in providing outstanding customer service, helped make the business profitable and I didn't want him to leave."

They share different areas of business: Michael is in charge of personnel, marketing, and education. Nate is in charge of the day-to-day operations and customer service.

Surprises

"There were only three of us for the first few years: myself, my girlfriend, and a mechanic. We worked in what I called a hole-in-the-wall. In 1988, I bought land and custom-built the repair shop and offices. The mechanic moved with me, my girlfriend didn't. That's when I decided not to hire close friends or family again. Our business grew into our new space quickly, and we started to be viewed as a successful repair shop; it was the first time that we ever got checks that bounced. I guess new customers saw us as a big, rich corporate company."

What Works

Michael and Nate are both highly compensated and share in the profits. Although they consult each other on important business decisions, they are very independent. It's a marriage of convenience. They share different areas of the business in which they both can shine and use their natural talents and expertise. They have a great deal of respect for each other, but they're not chummy.

As Michael explains, " I don't recommend being a business partner with a friend, because you may discover a side of your friend you didn't know, wouldn't know about otherwise, and may not like. Be aware that your friendship may be stressed as a result of business."

Key to Success

"We share a passion for doing the absolute best, quality work. We're both Type A personalities, bright, and aggressive. It is also great to have someone else on the team to be the buffer zone, someone you both trust. That's our office manager, who always has a wise perspective on things."

Friends and Partners: Case 1

Alasdair Clements and Nathan Withrington founded GoCar Rentals, Inc., in 2004 in San Francisco. They offer self-guided tours from Fisherman's Wharf and Union Square using a custom GPS software they developed that is packaged with very cute, small, yellow cars that are ideal for getting around in a busy city.

Alasdair firmly believes that to grow your business fast you need to have a partner. His research showed that there is an 80 percent failure rate for a sole proprietor and only a 30 percent failure rate with a partner. He also agrees with most entrepreneurs I have talked to that partners' skills, personalities, and talents must compliment each other. On the emotional side, both of us wanted out of corporate America and to build a business of our own.

Partnership Roles

It is essential to have strengths in different areas of the business. Nathan is the engineer and mechanic who secured the distributorship for "GoCars" in the United States. Alasdair considers himself an accidental entrepreneur because at first, he was brought in to write the business plan and formulate a financial projection for Nathan. He provided Nathan with benchmarks and risk management information so that he would know what he was getting into in the business. As they developed the idea and plans more, Alasdair realized he was helping to shape and adapt the vision and build the business in such a way as to differentiate it from his competitors in the tour industry. Alasdair subsequently became a partner and now handles the business side, marketing, public relations, personnel and they both oversee the day-to-day operations.

Surprises

Without trying, they made the front page of the business section of the *New York Times* within the first three months. With a trusted counter manager and Nathan handling the mechanical and maintenance and troubleshooting of the GoCars, Alasdair was freed up to think about growing the business. It was his decision to open another office in Union Square. After much research, analysis, and some trepidation, they opened another office. The big learning for Alasdair was to trust his intuition and decision-making process, because now the new location brings in 35 percent of their business in San Francisco.

What Works

Alasdair helps Nathan with strategic and objective decisions for the business. Both partners are flexible in their thinking; and can change and adapt quickly to market pressures. It is essential that they are both able to take the pulse of what's going on in the marketplace and take calculated risks to stay on the cutting edge in their industry. It is also very important for both partners to be willing to learn and grow as leaders and learn how to manage employees well.

Keys to Success

It is essential to trust each other and have similar business ethics. Communicate and collaborate on decisions and stick with your agreements as to your roles. It is also important to continually develop an understanding of others—both employees and customers. Perseverance and motivation to succeed are also keys.

Friends and Partners: Case 2

Anthony Sandberg and Richard Jepsen are the founder and CEO respectively of OCSC Sailing Club, Inc., in Berkeley, California. They started with one boat, a telephone, and a small office next to the Berkeley garbage dump.

Anthony and Richard have been friends and business partners for twenty-eight years. Anthony founded the company and Richard came aboard as a manager in the second year. Anthony offered Richard a fifty-fifty partnership because he saw his potential, and he wanted him to stay with the company.

Partnership Roles

Anthony explains, "I knew early on that two of me would be a disaster! I'm visionary, optimistic, charismatic, and I love working with people. I appreciate, respect, and consider everyone who walks through our door as friends. We are both master sailors and instructors who inspire confidence in those we teach or join us for a sail on the Bay or an adventure travel trip. Rich is organized, detailed, smart, and makes things work. He has systematized our processes so that they are repeatable and we can easily train others to run the day-to-day operations of the business."

Richard, the current CEO, says:

"I was both entranced by and knew I could enhance Anthony's vision, and I realized I had a knack for all aspects of the sailing school business. My desire, interest, and enthusiasm for getting my hands in the clay of this young business motivated me. I marveled at Anthony's creative thinking with the ability to think out of the box and make connections at a high level."

Richard's role is to keep his eye on continuous business growth, recognizing obstacles, seeing the downside, identifying possible hidden problems, and preparing for the worst-case scenario. According to Richard: "Anthony is the new ideas guy: 'Gee whiz, wouldn't it be great if we did this?' His personality, generosity, and sincere interest in others draws people to the school and club. Also, he has great credibility with his reputation as a well-traveled world-class sailor and adventurer. That's how we started our latest venture a few years ago: Adventure travel. His love of people, personality, and charisma is also our best marketing strategy."

Surprises

Richard continues: "A few years into the business we partnered with a psychologist who did team-building training for corporations. Anthony and I partnered on developing the experiential side of the training. Teaching corporate managers and employees to sail together was a wonderful experiential demonstration of what they were learning in the 'classroom,' and it was fun! It was instantly successful. Corporate events are still part of our business."

What Works

"We are first friends, and for better or worse this is the filter through which we have made business decisions," says Richard. "Generally, this has been a key to our business success. Certainly, at times we may have subverted the business' interests for the sake of being too patient with each other and flexible with each other's performance. In a long-term partnership, everything comes with a price. Yet since our first year, our business has been continually growing. We have a good match of skills and personalities. Our strengths compliment each other."

Keys to Success

The keys are our friendship, a good match of skills, respect for each other, and having fun. As Richard says, "From the beginning we have both been honest about the good, the bad, and the ugly about our business."

Family Partners: Case 1

Jim and Mary Germain are a husband-and-wife team who own a bed and breakfast, The Castle Valley Inn in Moab, Utah. After many years in the hospitality industry, it is a second career for Jim as he looks toward retirement. Mary, after many years as a homemaker, has stepped back into the workforce.

Partnership Roles

As Jim explains, "We do different things. We have a large property so I'm the yard-and-building maintenance guy. I often tell the guests that Mary is the boss because she is the first contact with guests. Mary does the Internet marketing, handles reservations and booking, plans menus, shops for food, and cooks breakfast. In addition, she also keeps the books. It really works for us to divide up the work. We both greet and chat with the guests and we really love that."

Surprises

The work is 24/7 and more physical than they expected, but they really enjoy it most of the time! There is little separation between work and the rest of their life. It is also gratifying to be appreciated by so many guests. Several consider the bed and breakfast their home away from home.

What Works

Jim and Mary equally share the workload and decisions. They like the challenge of learning new things and supporting each other. Both partners enjoy people and are willing to pitch in without resentment to help with the other person's "area" of the business. They enjoy each other's company. They both consider their bed and breakfast another adventure in their life. When they were in their twenties they spent two years traveling and camping in their car in South America and Africa. For them, it is a lifestyle choice. It also makes a big difference that they have other investments, savings, and are not solely dependent on the bed and breakfast for income.

Keys to Success

It is essential to build relationships not only with clients but with neighbors, and to contribute to the community. It also helps to be easygoing and adaptable to change.

Family Partners: Case 2

Christopher Brown and Christian Brown are a father-and-son team who run Golden Snail Builders. Currently they remodel family-owned residential properties in Oakland, California. Christopher says, "I really didn't think about bringing Christian on as a partner. But as projects came along, I needed help, and Christian became my primary worker and support. As his skills developed, I realized that he had the technical skills, the interpersonal skills, and the potential to run the whole project. I also enjoyed mentoring him, and it became natural to take him on as a partner."

Partnership Roles

The division of labor and roles must be clear so that the partners are carrying their own weight and feel good about it. Christian says, "We don't have a strict division of labor, it flows according to who has the best skill and talent set for what is needed at the time. For example, I'm much stronger physically than my dad." Christian is excellent at building and supervising foundations; Christopher is excellent at negotiating contracts and doing fine carpentry, as well as managing the overall project in terms of timing and logistics.

Surprises

The only surprise is how easy it is to work together. There is just no drama. Both men say that they are able to go with the flow and share the sheer enjoyment of collaborating on design.

What Works

Christopher and Christian share a mutual respect and a good solid work ethic. If one of the partners isn't carrying his weight, resentment builds and then problems occur. Christopher says, "So far, our willingness to communicate clearly without blaming each other has helped the projects go smoothly. Also, we both have a similar sense of humor, so we like to kid the crew and we all have fun. It's also important to always keep the goal in mind so that there is efficient teamwork and acknowledgment of each other's accomplishments." Christopher and Christian say their motto is: Keep it real, keep it fair, and keep it fun!

15 "Partnership is about trusting your partner and his or her business ethics, as well as appreciating and acknowledging each other's talents and skills."

Keys to Success

Partnership is about trusting your partner and his or her business ethics, as well as appreciating and acknowledging each other's talents and skills. These are the foundation of success. Also, each partner must be willing to be open to listening to all sides of an issue in order to resolve it fairly and quickly. Open communication is essential. We need to be able to see the goal outside of our own opinions and pull ourselves out of the issues to see the bigger picture as to what's best for the project or business.

When considering a partnership, remember these key learnings:

- Save heartbreak and money by writing a partnership agreement before you join forces.

- Be willing to learn and grow as a leader, especially when managing employees.

- Make sure that you and your partner complement each other in your strengths, roles, and skills.

- It is essential that you have similar business ethics and share a passion for quality.

- Open and honest communication is key to the health of any business.

Why a Business Plan?

DO THE FOLLOWING STATEMENTS sound familiar to you?

"Why do I need a business plan?"

"Since I'm financing my own business, I don't need a plan because I'm not going to ask the bank for a loan."

"I know what I want to do with my business this year. I don't need to write it down."

"I know I should do it, but I don't have time to write a business plan."

So, what is a business plan? A business plan is basically a document that precisely defines your business, identifies your business objectives, describes your strategies to reach the business objectives, and includes key financials, such as a balance sheet and a profit-and-loss statement.

Most people who are starting out or already in business think that writing a business plan is hard work. Well, they're right, it is—but it's worth it. When

16

"When you do a business plan, you are creating a very specific blueprint to help you make sound business decisions and help your business prosper. After all, would you build a house without a blueprint?"

you do a business plan, you are creating a very specific blueprint to help you make sound business decisions and help your business prosper. After all, would you build a house without a blueprint? A business plan gives you a time line, identifies resources, outlines your goals, and details your finances and marketing plan. Having a plan can make a big difference in terms of your business success, so get your business idea out of your head and put it in writing.

A business plan gives you the following advantages:

- It helps you take an objective look at the viability of your idea.

- It clarifies your thinking and channels your energy.

- It helps you define and outline your objectives and detailed plans.

- It focuses attention on important issues and helps you set priorities.

- It keeps everyone in your company focused on your vision.

- It can be used as a feasibility study for start-up or growth.

- It can be used as a benchmark to track performance.

- It can be used as a financial proposal to present to families, banks, or investors.

I recommend writing a business plan every year. I use a simple one to two page format and I love it because it is so easy to implement. I review it once a month. I always add a budget for financials. At first, I did a traditional business plan and never looked at it. When I hired someone to do the fancy one, I couldn't figure out how to use it, so it sat on the shelf. The plan helps me set benchmarks for the year—my objectives and goals. Throughout the year, I know exactly what I want to do and how I'm measuring up to my goals. The beauty is also that I can change it. It's a living document.

—**Cindy Elwell,** Divorce with Dignity, Alameda, California

Keep Your Business Plan Simple

Most often, a simple business plan will do. The only time you need an extensive business plan is when your goal is to obtain financing, in which case make sure that you fulfill all the requirements requested by the lender or investors. Otherwise, there is no need for your plan to be long and elaborate. Your vision of your business is the foundation. Imagine what your business will look like in three years. Your plan then becomes the blueprint for how to make your vision a reality and get your company where you want it to go.

To keep your plan as simple as possible, answer these basic questions:

1. What are my product, program, and service offerings?

2. What is my prospective target market?

3. Who are my competitors?

4. What key benefits do I offer so that customers will choose to do business with me?

Turn the answers to these questions into your mission statement, your goals, the strategies to reach your goals, and specific projects along with dates for completion. Here are some suggestions for writing your business plan.

• *Write a business plan every year.* The first year you are in business, your plan will reflect your best guess, based on your market research, knowledge of your industry, and product or service you offer. Your first plan will take the longest to write, but it will become a prototype for the plans that follow. The following year, writing your plan will be easier because you simply revise your original plan. You can see what worked, what didn't, and how to develop more achievable goals and accurate time lines.

• *Ask for help, but do not have someone else write the entire plan for you.* If you do, you won't develop the direct, hands-on relationship with your business that you need. However, you do not need to write the plan alone. Involve members of your staff. Ask for feedback from colleagues. Hire a consultant to keep you on track.

• *Don't spend more time than you need on your business plan.* It doesn't need to take days to write.

• *Print copies of your business plan for everyone in your organization.* Make sure that everyone reads it, understands it, and gets behind it. Treat it like a living document. If the time line proves to be unreasonable three months into the year, revise it and adjust the completion dates. One purpose of the plan is to help you track how well you are doing what you said you were going to do.

Use consultants, resources, and books to help you write a business plan. One of the most helpful books is *The One Page Business Plan* by Jim Horan. It is written in a workbook format and simplifies the process. Figure 3-1 is a sample "One Page Business Plan." Although it is intended for a consultant, it also fits most nonconsultant microbusinesses.

Target Your Market!

ONCE YOU HAVE DONE your exploratory market research, you are ready to zero in on your particular target market. The following exercise will help you clarify the best segment(s) within your target market for your product or service.

TARGET MARKET WORKSHEET

1. Questions to Help Determine Your Customer Target Market(s)

"Who are my customers? What do I know about them (i.e., economic level, lifestyle, sex and age range, income level, buying habits)?"

_____

"Where are my customers located? Where do they live, work, and currently shop? What problems do they want solved?"

_____

"What is the projected size of the market? What percentage of the total market could be mine?"

_____

"What do my customers both need and want?"

_____

"How can I meet those needs? What are the specific ways in which my business will benefit my customers?"

_____

Figure 3-1

The HR Consulting Group

Sally McKenzie & Bob Wilson

FY2007 Consolidated Plan

vision

Within the next 3 years grow The HR Consulting Group into a $1 million North Texas consulting and training company specializing in human resource training and consulting services for companies within a 50 mile radius of Dallas/Ft. Worth that have between 50 and 500 employees.

mission

Bring Preventative HR Programs to Growing Companies!

objectives

- Achieve 2007 sales of $ 350,000.
- Earn pre-tax profits of $75,000; after paying two partner salaries of $100,000.
- Consistently have partners bill out 6 days per month at $1,500 per day.
- Generate $40,000 from audits & assessments.
- Increase training program & product revenue from $7,500 a month to $10,000 by Aug. 30th.
- Increase ave. bi-weekly attendance at employer council meetings from 12 to 20 by May 15th.
- Produce six notable, publishable case studies in 2007.
- Take a minimum of 2 one-week vacations in the next twelve months.

strategies

- Become known for preventing catastrophic employee problems that destroy businesses.
- Attract clients with 50 to 500 employees, business owners who want preventive solutions.
- Promote initial trial through our monthly employer council meetings & low-cost guide books.
- Generate revenues thru preventive audits & assessments, training programs & consulting.
- Use technology/Internet for tele-classes, audits & assessments, & selling training guides.
- Strategically align our firm w/ local employment law attorneys, CPAs & business consultants.
- Continue to create books, guides, audiotapes, & assessment products from existing services.
- Build a business that is ultimately not dependent on my presence; which will make it sellable.

action plans

- Publish "Employer's Bill of Rights Handbook" by Feb. 28th.
- Complete Sexual Harassment, Family Leave & Diversity Guidebooks by April 20th.
- Launch "New Manager Training Series" May 1st; repeat program once in Q3 & Q4.
- Begin hosting monthly "Managers Problem Solving Roundtable" in July.
- Complete makeover of website & e-commerce systems by Sept. 30th.
- Introduce Smart System's web-employee appraisal process to our clients starting Nov. 1st.

"What is unique about my business? Why will these customers buy from me?"

"What does my product/service/idea offer to a marketplace that has somehow managed without it so far?" (*Note*: This is a key issue for innovative entrepreneurs.)

17 "A key question to help determine your customer target market(s) is, "What does my product/service/idea offer to a marketplace that has somehow managed without it so far?"

2. Key Questions to Ask, Based on Your Research

"Is there sufficient market potential for my business to be successful?"

"Do I and/or my company possess the expertise and resources needed to create the required products and services? If not, what would I need and how would I obtain it?"

"Is there enough profit potential?"

Put Your Own Money on the Line: Investing and Financing

WHENEVER MY SON ASKS me to buy something expensive for him, I always ask him one question before I decide whether to buy it: "Would you be willing to spend your own allowance money on this?" The key words here are "willing" and "your own money." If he says yes, I will consider his request seriously. Why? Because this is something he really wants, not something he thinks might be cool to own. Because he wants it enough to put his money where his mouth is.

This is a key question to ask yourself when you are considering starting your own business. If your business is funded with your own hard-earned money rather than other people's money, your chance of succeeding goes way up. According to the Small Business Administration (sba.gov), "more than 80 percent of new entrepreneurs start their businesses without any commercial loans or debt financing. In order to not saddle themselves with debt, they often choose to obtain their initial financing from their own savings, from friends and family members, informal investors, or home equity loans."

Funding a business with your own money means that you will not go into business on a whim or just try it to see how it goes. It means that you have limited financial resources of money, and you know what it took to earn it. Your first business expense probably won't be a fancy new car. Perhaps it will be a new computer and an accounting system instead. After all, you have limited money, time, and energy to invest in your

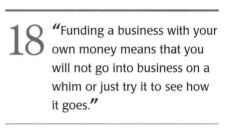

18 *"Funding a business with your own money means that you will not go into business on a whim or just try it to see how it goes."*

business, and you need all three to succeed—each week, month, and year.

Questions to Consider

Whatever source of financing you use, here are questions to consider when you are doing your financial planning for your new business:

- What will your start-up costs be?

- Will there be slow seasons each year? How will customers pay you—every 30 days, 60 days, 90 days, or on some other basis?

- What kind of variable expenses do you project (e.g., direct labor, materials, commissions, advertising)?

- What will your fixed expenses be (e.g., rent, utilities, leased equipment, insurance, payroll)?

- What salary or owner's draw do you need each month to support yourself? Your salary or draw should be enough to cover your monthly budgeted fixed expenses, such as your mortgage, rent, car payments, food, etc. *Rule of thumb*: It's best to have six months to one year of living expenses available for your first year of business.

* What is your best estimate of your sales and expenses, month by month, for the first year of your business? What is your break-even projection? Your profit projection?

Once you have run the numbers for your new business based on questions like those above, ask yourself, "How long will it take to achieve my break-even point?" Then ask, "How long will it take me to make my projected profit once I reach my break-even point?" Be conservative.

* In the first year of business, how realistic is it for you to attract the number of customers you need to break even and make a profit?

* How many clients do you need to see a month?

* How many widgets do you need to sell a month?

You will be surprised how many items you need to sell just to break even. In order to make a profit, you need to sell a whole lot more than that. For example, if you are a consultant working from your home office and you've figured that your overhead is $2,000/month and you want an income of $60,000 annually, or $5,000/month the first year, this means that you need to have $7,000 worth of billable hours/month. If you charge $100 per hour, you need to have seventy client-hours a month, or 3.5 client-hours per day.

New entrepreneurs say, "Yes! I would love to work only 3.5 hours per day!" However, what will it actually take to generate this number of client-hours? Depending on your business, it might take two hours of marketing for one hour of billable work, especially when you're in the start-up phase. Add in slow times of the year (such as the Christmas holidays), administrative time, and the fact that you are probably doing all the business tasks yourself during the first year, and you will discover that you probably won't have much time to lounge by the pool.

However, there might be a time when you need to finance your business, either through a bank loan or investors—in other words, a time when you need a large sum of money that you can't pull out of your business or savings. Common reasons for financing include inventory costs, purchase and repair of equipment and fixed assets, and working capital shortages. If you want to retain total control in running your business, obtain debt financing—a loan from a bank, family, or friends. Another option is equity financing, in which you give investors a percentage of your business profits and/or a say in how to manage your business in return for their money.

Start out on the right foot by keeping good records. Accurate record keeping is an essential element in measuring the success of your business. Opening a separate business account for all business-related earnings and expense transactions will enable you to track your spending habits and budget your expenses. It is also a useful tool in planning a marketing strategy. Tracking your income stream allows you to better recognize seasonal earning trends.

—**Diane Tyler,** D. L. Tyler & Associates, Oakland, CA

Careful planning and realistic financial projections can make or break your business. To be truly successful, you need to pay close attention to the details in order to sustain your business and reach the profits you envision.

CHAPTER 4

WHAT DO YOU BRING — TO THE PARTY?

What Motivates You to Keep Going?

AS I WATCHED the fireworks last July 4th, it struck me that Independence Day—which marks the birth of our country, in 1776 a struggling, intrepid, individualistic new nation—embodies the entrepreneurial spirit. The Declaration of Independence, symbolizing the motivation to build a country that promotes "life, liberty and the pursuit of happiness," reminds me of the mission statement that new entrepreneurs struggle to write when they are giving "birth" to a business venture—a daunting task filled with challenges and risks, yet exciting and full of hope. Just as our entrepreneurial forefathers were determined to build a new life for themselves in America, today's entrepreneurs are highly motivated to succeed.

Clearly, making money is a large motivation. Aside from making money, though, what motivates you to go into your own business?

Once I gave a talk at a conference on the four most common motivators for entrepreneurs: Creativity, Control, Challenge, and Cash. The audience responded by spontaneously suggesting other words beginning with the letter "C" that motivated them in their work. Since then, I have been thinking about and experiencing these motivators in my own business and my work with clients. Here is my list of motivational "C" words and how each impacts the entrepreneurial lifestyle. I invite you to define each word in the way that's most meaningful to you.

Challenge

If *challenge* is your motivator, you love the exhilaration of succeeding at a particularly hard task, inventing a new product, or finding a fun way to market your service. You like to work on projects that provide opportunities to try new approaches. You love learning and are willing to take calculated risks frequently.

For example, Barbara Llewellyn of Barbara Llewellyn Catering in Oakland, California, says, "After twenty years in business, I still have challenges in my biz. I like that. It is always a moving target to know exactly how to promote my business and continue doing well. Things change in the market all the time, and I need to be on my toes. I just love to take on something new—client, product, and type of event. I am truly excited about working with a new or repeat client, making it happen, creating the event and then moving on to the next!"

Control

If *control* is your primary motivator, you want to be the lead dog. You're a take-charge kind of person. You are interested in every aspect of your business. Often the lines between business and play are blurred because you are your business.

For example, Hugh Groman of Hugh Groman Catering, Inc., in Berkeley, California, says, "I am passionate about food and I love all aspects of business. I knew early in my twenties that it was not my natural state to work for others. It feels totally normal to be the rainmaker, take calculated risks, to challenge myself to develop the best product and customer service as well as direct others—basically to be in charge. I have the vision and know what I want to create and choose people to be around me who can buy in and make it happen."

Creativity

If *creativity* is your motivator, you are innovative and independent, with high energy and strong self-confidence. You also like to tackle situations or problems and find creative ways to solve them. You thrive on tackling projects that might involve unknown difficulties or have outcomes that are unpredictable.

Pauline Pearsall of Pauline Pearsall, Inc., a staging company, says, "I'm a pathological optimist. I simply have confidence that everything will work out. I started in business accidentally after a career in social work. I just wanted to get back to using my creativity. So I did slipcovers, catering, and staging. I realized what I liked about all three was the visual presentation so I decided to focus exclusively on staging homes for sale. I have developed tried-and-true systems, especially when I have multiple houses to be staged simultaneously, but I love the variety and the creative challenge we face for each project large or small."

Cash

You love making lots of money and may also be motivated by achieving status and prestige. If *cash* is your number one motivator, choose a business that has a strong likelihood of growing fast. Otherwise, if you aren't making a healthy profit within the first two years, you'll lose interest.

For example, Michael Dennison of Bavarian Professionals, BMW Auto Repair, in Berkeley, California, agrees. Michael says, "Choose your business well. It must be one that can be profitable over time. If you have what I call a lifestyle business where lots of owners are spending fifty to sixty hours a week working and lots of people want to work in that business, chances are you can pay people less. However, customers also have lots of choices as to with whom to do business, and they can look for lower pricing. It's hard to make this type of business profitable over time. In addition, it is essential to be able to compensate your key people well in salary and profit sharing. This will free up your time because your managers are motivated to build the business as much as you are. My business is growing considerably each year and I have been working twenty hours a week for the last five years."

Contribution

If *contribution* is your primary motivator, you want to make a difference or help others improve their lives in both personal and practical ways. This could be anything from founding a nonprofit, to providing direct aid to third-world countries, to being an auto mechanic who goes out of his way to make an emergency repair on a customer's car.

Anthony Sandberg of OCSC Sailing Club, Inc., in Berkeley, California, says, "I've been in business here for thirty years, starting with one sailboat and living in my car for the first few months. I believe in giving back to the community in any way I can. Since we've had our clubhouse, we have made it available for fundraisers for local groups, nonprofits, pretty much any of our members or their friends who ask. We also regularly contribute gift certificates for sailing lessons to local auction fundraisers. In addition, we support our employees by putting some through college, helping them with a down payment for a house, whatever is needed. I love the work and the people I work with. I have a very successful business, but if I had to close my doors tomorrow and walk away without a cent, I'd say 'Boy, those were thirty well-spent years!'"

Competition

If *competition* is your primary motivator, you want to be the best at what you do. Being competitive in the marketplace is essential to keeping your business doors open, but for you it is also a strong internal motivator. You strive to be the market leader in your field.

Alasdair Clements of GoCar Tours, Inc., in San Francisco, California, says, "We want to grow big. After three years in business, we're still figuring out who besides tourists and locals are part of our potential market. We feel we have only 10 percent of our actual market. We opened a second location in San Francisco that now brings in 35 percent of our business in this area and we have two franchise locations in the United States. Yet, we would also like to expand internationally. We are building a brand that is recognized nationally and internationally. We always need to be one step ahead of our competitors."

Collaboration

If *collaboration* is your primary motivator, you enjoy developing a special synergy with a group of colleagues to create a strategic alliance or a new product or service. You want to brainstorm with trusted colleagues for inspiration, validation of your efforts, encouragement, and renewed energy. If you have employees, you will promote teamwork and a free exchange of ideas.

For example, several women entrepreneurs I interviewed for this book belong to the same business networking organization, Women Presidents Organization (WPO). All of them have noted that it's incredibly helpful to express what is going on in their business, get suggestions, and hear what other women have done. These entrepreneurs help each other by sharing different perspectives and ways of processing issues and problem solving. They feel that a support group or a business coach is very important for all business owners, especially women, so they don't feel that they are each alone on an island.

Business owners usually have two or three internal drivers that motivate them to start and run their own business. Of course, you need to be competitive and make a profit in order to have a viable business, but usually there are additional motivators that drive you. When I'm trying to find out what makes people tick I often ask, "What really excites you about what you do?" Answer that question for yourself,

19 *"You need to be competitive and make a profit in order to have a viable business, but usually there are additional motivators that drive you."*

and you'll know what your strongest motivators are. Apply those to your business, and you have a great chance of succeeding at something you love doing.

Entrepreneurs are people who are highly motivated to succeed. All motivation is internally driven, and each person usually has two to three strong motivators. In the following exercise choose your strong motivators from the list below and write your own definitions for each (if your strong motivators do not appear on this list, add them in the additional spaces provided):

What Are Your Key Motivators?

CASH _____

CREATIVITY _____

CHALLENGE _____

COLLABORATION _____

CONTROL _____

COMPETITION _____

CONTRIBUTION _____

Others:

_____

_____

Next, describe how your key motivators might complement each other to create optimal satisfaction and productivity in your business:

_____

_____

_____

_____

If You're the Boss, Who Keeps You Accountable?

WHEN YOU WORK for someone else, you may not always appreciate having a boss. Yet one good thing about a boss is that this person keeps you on track and accountable. But who keeps you accountable when you are your own boss?

Let's look at what it means to be accountable. The dictionary defines *accountability* as "considered to be responsible and answerable." In other words: You're in charge. You get to take the credit (and the blame) for what happens in your business.

It's no wonder that the most frequent reason given for starting a business is "being my own boss"—fulfilling the dream of pursuing your own ideas and being in control rather than under someone else's control. Once you're in business for yourself, however, you realize that along with the control comes accountability. When the going gets tough—and it will—will you opt for the beach? Or will you be accountable by pushing on with the business of your business? This means dealing with all the nuts and bolts of growing a business: writing and reviewing your business or marketing plan, learning your product better, minding your accounting, keeping up with market trends, adding skills, staying visible in your field, achieving your goals, and, where applicable, keeping your investors happy.

Here's a simple system you may want to adopt to achieve your goals so that you can be accountable to your business and still go to the beach—but without a guilty conscience:

- *Think it*: Decide what you need to accomplish, and set priorities for your objectives.

- *Write it*: In a journal, write your goals and put your action steps, or tasks, into the categories listed below. This gets your plans out of your head and onto paper and into action.

- *Speak it*: Tell at least three people you see regularly what you plan to do. At some point, you will see one of those people, and they'll ask: "How's your new product going?" This makes your plan real and motivates you to follow through.

- *Complete it*: Set completion dates for each task in each category. If you know what your tasks are and when you want to have them done, you are much more likely to do them. I can't tell you how powerful this is. Thinking is the beginning of

20 "Every great accomplishment starts with an idea or thought. When you write down your thoughts, ideas, and plans, they become more real and actionable."

possibility. Every great accomplishment starts with an idea or thought. When you write down your own thoughts, ideas, and plans, they become more real and actionable. If you add telling people about your plans, you increase your accountability. This motivates you to meet your goals.

The following four categories provide one way to set priorities for necessary tasks:

1. *I have to do it now.* These are things you must do right away, or you'll suffer serious consequences, like losing that big account.

2. *Important, but I can do it later.* This category may include a thank-you note to a colleague who referred business to you, updating your website, or preparing for a sales presentation.

3. *I have to do it regularly.* These are the maintenance and clerical tasks that need to be done. However, don't let yourself get bogged down with them. Schedule a certain amount of time during the week to do these tasks, and stick to it.

4. *It's a time waster.* These are tasks that others want you to do, but which are not your top priority. They include that stuff on your desk that you think you might use someday, but haven't looked at for months. These are the tasks you can take off your "to-do" list.

At different times, the same task can fit into any of these categories. For example, I have one talk that I give frequently. Each time I give it, I change it slightly to fit the audience. Consequently, I have several renditions of the agenda, overheads, and handouts.

The first time I made this presentation, this task fell into the top category, "I have to do it now." After I'd given the talk ten times, the presentation materials fell into the "Important, but I can do it later" category. However, when I was about to give this presentation recently, it fell into the "I have to do it now" category again because I needed to totally reorganize the materials into a new notebook.

Now the presentation materials fall into the "I have to do it regularly" category, because I can update them very easily and quickly. Before I reorganized the materials, however, they fell into the "It's a time waster" category because I had to sort through a pile of materials each time I gave the presentation.

Magic Formula: Intuition and Intention

HAVE YOU EVER NOTICED that you have a small inner voice of guidance? This is your intuition. Perhaps you've heard this inner voice during meditation, or when you're driving, or perhaps just after you wake up in the morning. Some of my most creative inspirations occur while I'm in the shower!

When I listen I have trust and faith that my intention for my business will happen. I am clear this inner guidance or intuition is my business partner! It's easy when business is going well, but it's harder to follow your own inner guidance when business and/or your life is challenging.

For example, I once had three projects canceled at the same time through no fault of mine. What I have learned to do is to ask: What is the learning here? What might be open to me that wouldn't have been if I were busy with those projects?

I am able to give myself the gift of focus, I have renewed energy to move forward even though my business expectations were not met. In this case, I realized that I had been doing these same three projects in similar venues many times before. It was time to stretch myself in a new way. I took the time to develop talks with the message from this book, and many opportunities opened for paid speaking engagements.

This is the magic I'm talking about. Intention is connected with your passion. You can see it, taste it, and feel it, but you're not sure how you'll get what you're aiming for. When your purpose becomes clear, you can align it with your vision for your business and the magic starts happening—achieving your intention seems much easier and in some cases effortless. Sounds good, but how do you do it?

Opportunities continually appear or show up in business. The key is to recognize them and act on them. When you have clarity of purpose and know what you want, it is much easier to know which opportunities will further your vision.

That's why I recommend that you SCAN for opportunities, SCOUT for new learnings, experiment and test, try different options and STEER in the direction that best fits your vision. As I see it:

21 *"When your purpose becomes clear, you can align it with your vision for your business and the magic starts happening."*

INTENTION = Clearly Focused CHOICE.

Going with the Flow

As a business owner you need to take a vacation at least once a year—for rest, relaxation, and rejuvenation. For example, every year my family goes to a family camp in the Sierra foothills in California. One day while floating on my raft in the local river near camp, I had a revelation. No one was there except me and the magnificence of nature. I was floating, not steering. Wow! I had set my course—floating yet knowing I could steer myself away from the waterfall or tangle of weeds or rocks at any time.

I kept my awareness alert and relaxed into the bliss of floating. I was going with the flow, where the current was taking the raft, with me on it. Yet all it took was a few hand paddles and I could steer in another direction without fear or effort. Floating is a great metaphor for intention. It doesn't mean taking the path of least resistance. But it is a metaphor for clarifying your direction as specifically as possible, and then making adjustments as you move along—manifesting your intention. Challenges come along (like getting tangled in the weeds), but you make adjustments and move on. As with the raft, you can control the paddle but not the current. Hardly anyone or any form of transportation reaches the destination in a straight line: A sailboat tacks, a train goes around or through mountains, etc. Keep your intention or destination in sight and in your heart. Just keep going with the flow. If you bump into an obstacle, it's a reminder to re-evaluate and choose what's next.

Resistance

But when you are not going with the flow, fear arises—which is your resistance. It shows up for me even though I have chosen my direction, the project, or the talk I'm going to give. Why? Because it means change and not knowing how I'm going to make it happen. It can stop me in my tracks! I love this unofficial definition of *fear*: **F**alse **E**vidence **A**ppearing **R**eal.

When fear stops you, take one baby step toward your intention and keep moving one step at a time. Energy begins to build, support shows up, and soon you are on your way. I am better able to listen to my intuition, that inner guidance whispering encouragement. *Remember*: Intention only becomes real through clarity and doing something about it! Take the steps to manifest your intention and allow it to happen.

Magic

Magic is the taking action part. Put magic in your goals. This is what Magic stands for:

M = **M**easurable

A = **A**ct on to-do list daily

G = **G**oals give your dream a deadline

I   = **I**nspire others to assist you

C = **C**onfidence and belief in yourself and your abilities

You can do it. Take these magic steps and allow it to happen. Also your clear intention is like an umbrella, a safe shelter for new thinking, out-of-the-box ideas, creative expression as well as the space for attracting resources, expertise, and whatever it takes to bring your intention into reality.

Even knowing all this, you may be tempted to give up because it isn't working the way you planned or intended. I find one way to get unstuck is to choose an inspirational quote or saying. The quote always seems to be just what I need to hear for encouragement or inspiration. I also use this when I am making an important decision. I have all the pertinent information to make an informed choice. This is when I like to check in with my inner guidance.

Try this simple exercise:

Ask yourself: "What do I choose at this moment?"
Hold that thought.
Say out loud what you choose in this moment.
Invite yourself to think of the very next step for you to take to allow this choice,
    insight, or intention to happen.
Write it down.

Now, try this meditation:

Gently close your eyes. Begin to relax. Take in a deep breath.
Release all judgments about the day, breathe in peace and harmony.
With your next breath, let go of the tension in your body.
Focus on your feet and relax.
Release any tension in your lower back.
Feel your neck and shoulders—let them all go.
Notice any tightness in your jaw; release and relax.
Feel the seat beneath you. Let the full weight of your body relax down into the floor
    and feel the connection between you and mother earth.
Now, rest in the moment. Follow your natural breath. (Look into your heart and see
    what guiding thoughts may arise. Allow yourself to relax into the peaceful,
    embracing silence.)

Be in this silence for ten minutes.
Slowly start bringing your attention back into the room. Hold in your heart that still
small voice of guidance.
When you are ready, open your eyes.

This is the magic of synergy: Set your intention, trust, and take action.
Most entrepreneurs think they have to connect all the dots, but when they get
and keep the energy going, it just happens all by itself.

Remember to listen to your own intuition and inner guidance. It works.

Making Procrastination Work for You

PROCRASTINATION IS THE OPPOSITE of time management. Solo business
owners must juggle shifting priorities daily. They are the ultimate practition-
ers of multitasking. How do they do it? The answer is they don't—not always.
They procrastinate. Being your own boss is great—until you realize that you
are the only one who truly knows what your weekly To Do list contains. It's
easy to tell yourself that you'll do it tomorrow.

I suggest that you put into your weekly plan both the practice of time
management and of conscious procrastination, and establish an accountability system that will help you check off items on your To Do list—and still
have some fun. Think of procrastination as a way to build balance into your
life. A tongue-in-cheek definition of an entrepreneur is someone who would
rather work 80 hours a week for himself than 40 hours a week for someone
else. But sometimes those 60 to 80 hours turn into 90 hours, with at least 5 to
10 hours wasted on procrastination. Instead of worrying about procrastinat-
ing, put open space in your calendar to create time to do things you like that
are unrelated to work. Worry makes you anxious and unproductive. Open
time allows you to do things you like. It can be a time for creativity, for relaxation, and to help you feel rejuvenated.

One of my clients recently decided to read a novel for thirty minutes each
day. In the first week, she managed to read the novel for two hours on Sunday
and fifteen minutes on Tuesday, Thursday, and Friday. She acknowledged that
she didn't reach her goal, but she had gotten started. By the second week, she
read thirty minutes each day except on Saturday and Sunday. By the third

week, she was so hooked on the novel that she read one hour every day and finished the book. I asked her whether reading the book helped or hindered her work schedule. To her surprise, she said that she got more done for her business in the third week. Upon reflection, she realized that she was more focused and efficient the third week because she wanted to continue reading the book and didn't waste time thinking about getting her work done; she just did it. There is an old saying: If you want something done, ask a busy person to do it.

Procrastination has a negative connotation, but here's how you can make it work for you: On Sunday evening or Monday morning, write your To Do list for the week. Decide how much time you normally procrastinate. Allow two hours for pure procrastination, according to your regular modus operandi. Then decide what you would like to do that week that is not related directly to your business. Prioritize your workload for the week, estimate the hours needed to get it all done, and then determine how many hours you have left for "fun."

Next, divide that time into "family time," "social engagements," and your "private time." Don't worry about family time and social engagements; they will find their way into your calendar. Work with the amount of time you have left for "private time." Then schedule "private time" into your daily calendar as you see fit. You may find that some days you have thirty minutes before bedtime or twenty minutes on the commuter train or bus to work. Why not plan those times as carefully as you do your business meetings? The other way to do it is to leave the time open, so that you can do just what you feel like doing at that time.

For those of you who don't like so much structure, be ready to take advantage of unexpected free time. For example, last week I was preparing for a class I planned to teach the next week when I got a phone call telling me that the organization had decided not to offer the class for two more weeks. That phone call freed up my calendar for one evening that week and one the next week. So instead of

22 *"If you don't manage your time well, you may never actually enjoy those things you love to do."*

preparing for the class, I went out to dinner with friends, with whom I hadn't been able to get together for a while. If you don't manage your time well, you may never actually enjoy those things you love to do (besides growing your business).

What Stops You in Your Tracks: Self-Sabotage and Resistance

LET'S FACE IT: sometimes, although it's the last thing on your conscious mind, you sabotage your own plans. For example, you have a plan, but you aren't taking the action steps you need to follow through and reach your goal.

Why would people sabotage their own good intentions? Resistance, fear, and that voice inside that never has anything good to say to you about yourself! Perhaps you don't want to admit that you don't know how to do something, or perhaps you're not letting yourself do what it takes to sell yourself and your services.

Resistance

There are reasons why you resist what you really want. There are payoffs. It's much easier to keep doing what you already know how to do, what you're comfortable doing. People often choose safety and security over making changes because they don't want to face their feelings of fear and limitation. At least the current circumstances are familiar. It is a human habit to continue doing what you are used to doing, even if you don't like it, because it's the pattern you know.

23 *"It is a human habit to continue doing what you are used to doing, even if you don't like it, because it's the pattern you know."*

When you don't take a risk, you can couch your resistance in the guise of being "responsible," "practical," and "reliable."

Try this exercise to move you past your resistance:

1. Ask yourself: "How much do I want to stick with my belief that 'I can't do _____'"? Fill in the blank with your current "I can't."

2. Activity: What is the particular change you are contemplating, such as a new business opportunity, a new sales promotion, or a speaking engagement? Write it in the blank:

3. Loss vs. Gain: Make a list of everything you think you will lose or gain from this change.

Loss

_____

_____

_____

_____

Gain

_____

_____

_____

_____

Which list is longer? If your Loss list is much longer than your Gain list, perhaps you're better off not making this change. If your Gain list is at least as long as or longer than your Loss list, get off the couch and get going!

However, it's essential to re-evaluate your lists. For each item on your Loss list, ask yourself, "Am I willing to give this up?" And for each item on your Gain list, ask yourself, "How important is this item to me and my business?" Then ask yourself, "Are there any more items to add to my Gain list? Perhaps there is something you didn't put on the Gain list, because you felt it was too silly, too scary, or too huge? Put it on the list. Then, after this evaluation, if the payoff is worth the effort, keep going. When it's not, stop!

Make Friends with Your Inner Critic

Your Inner Critic is another big obstacle. Your Critic sabotages you constantly, saying things like:

"I need to stick with what I know best. I can't do this!"

"I'm not a good public speaker, and speaking is essential for this project."

"I don't have much to offer because I'm new in my field."

Sound familiar? You'll notice that the Critic comments on everything you do and everything you haven't done yet. One thing you can count on: The messages are always bad. The Inner Critic is bad news, because your brain believes what you tell it about yourself. It's very easy to believe those negative messages from your Critic, and you will act as if those messages are true.

The good news is that you can reprogram the Critic in your head to give you positive and supportive messages instead of negative and defeating ones.

Here's how:

- Tune into your Critic and listen to what its voice says. Write down some of the things your Critic says to you. Ask yourself: "Is that true?"

- Turn each criticism into an encouraging statement (often called an affirmation). For example, for the criticism "I'm not good at sales," untie the NOT. Now you have an affirmation: "I'm good at sales." For the criticism "I hate my work," pretend you are a computer and push the delete button. Now push the insert button and insert "My work is innovative."

- Write two or three affirmations on index cards. Say and write them on a daily basis. Try doing this ten to twelve times a day. You won't believe them at first. It takes practice and time to quiet your Inner Critic. But don't worry. You will begin to believe your positive self-talk.

- Practice your positive statements every day for a month. You'll be happily surprised at the results.

- Use "you" instead of "I" in your positive statement. For example, "You always know what to say." Why? Because it sounds like someone else is complimenting you and giving you support.

Invest in yourself by treating yourself as if you count. The number one reason people buy from you is that you are CONFIDENT! If you believe in you, so will your customers!

The Isolation of the "SoloPreneur"

ISOLATION IS ONE of the unforeseen difficulties encountered by the new entrepreneur, especially by consultants or home-based business folks. Once their business is running, entrepreneurs find themselves spending more time alone than expected. This is especially true for people who most recently worked in a large corporation. Those informal meetings, talks with colleagues, and team projects are not possible in their current setting.

They also discover they are spending time on administrative tasks that others used to handle. Often this additional workload cuts into the time that otherwise would be available to spend with family and friends. Growing the business comes first, and social activities get put on the back burner.

This is understandable—but it also adds to feeling isolated.

Making Supportive Connections

If this is true for you, the good news is: There is no need to be a lone wolf. Make connections and build a support network. You will find that this network will nurture you and your business in many unforeseen ways—not just with business referrals, but with new ideas, accountability, and solutions to problems, and with a safe group to talk about what's really going on in your business.

24 *"Make connections and build a support network. You will find that this network will nurture you and your business in many unforeseen ways."*

Solo piloting your entrepreneurial flight requires you to be committed to self-monitoring. Initially, when your blank date book is only full of potential, launch yourself by reciting daily affirmations. Dress as though you have a full day of appointments. Then, design and activate a detailed workday schedule with specific objectives. This infrastructure will sustain you as you move forward and transform your goals into achievements. You will soar on your newfound wings to amazing heights!

—**Margi Urquhart,** Realtor, Alpharetta, Georgia

One way to connect is to start your own business support group. In major cities there are many networking events and professional organizations that you can attend. These are good sources for developing contacts and creating an informal support group of your own. Invite one like-minded person to help you start a business support network.

The goal is for members to feel comfortable discussing all aspects of their business, setting goals, and providing accountability for each other. Request that your partner or colleague recruit one other business owner to join your group, and you do the same. Once you have at least four members, schedule your initial meeting at a convenient, neutral location. A local restaurant or coffeehouse works well because it eliminates one person always feeling responsible for providing the office and refreshments.

At the first meeting, form a consensus on the ground rules for your group and ask for a commitment of at least four months. Be specific about the needs and motivations of each member, so that everyone can see how this group will benefit them. A small group of four to six works best. Time and money are precious to new business owners. For a networking group to be successful, members need to see how spending time away from earning money benefits their business. It can't be just a nice social occasion to avoid feeling lonely.

My most successful business support group was formed to help each member market her business. We have been meeting once a month for six years. There are four women, all in private practice—career consulting, business coaching, bodywork, and psychotherapy. We still discuss marketing ideas, but it has evolved into much more. We cheer each other through our successes and support each other through our failures; we test out new ideas before we unveil them publicly; we set goals and keep each other accountable; we laugh, as well as share practical tips and contacts; and as a result, we have developed a mutual trust.

Your support network will develop its own character over time, keep you connected, and provide surprising benefits. If forming or participating in a network is not for you, try renting an office in a shared-services office building. There are many opportunities to schmooze with other business owners in the building, much like chatting with folks from other units in a large company.

You can also try talking weekly with a good friend. Tell each other your goals for the next week. Agree to check up on each other to see if you have achieved your goals. You can also hire a business coach to give you new perspectives, resources, ideas, and encouragement. Build regular exercise into your workweek—at the health club, on the tennis court, walking with a friend, or jogging on the beach. It gives you a change of pace, fresh air, and energy. No matter how busy you are, spend time with your family and friends every week. Attend social activities that you enjoy!

Join your local Chamber of Commerce, a trade association or specialized professional association, or a small business referral network. Serve on a committee, building contacts in your community. Go beyond "Let's exchange business cards." Get to know people, develop relationships, and offer assistance—and opportunities will naturally evolve. People want to refer business to people they know and trust.

Burnout: How to De-Stress

DO YOU LIE AWAKE at night feeling anxious, but you don't know why? Do you wake up in the morning and dread going to work? Is the excitement of being your own boss gone? Does this sound familiar? Doing something you love and being your own boss are probably the biggest reasons you chose self-employment. Yet the other side of the coin may be the stress you feel about meeting your own high expectations for business success.

Jeff, the owner of a successful small manufacturing company, was lying awake one night thinking about work, when he noticed that his body felt tense and rigid, and that his heart was beating rapidly. He was alarmed. "Why am I feeling so anxious?" Jeff asked himself. "I've just completed my best year in business, and my personal life is great. Yet why am I feeling physically ill?" The next day he saw his doctor, who confirmed that Jeff had high blood pressure. The doctor put him on medication with the suggestion that he take some time off and try to relax. As Jeff was leaving, he thought, "How can I do that?" Gradually, he realized that all along, he felt guilty about taking time off for himself. Consequently, he'd taken only two real vacations in ten years. After much soul-searching and careful analysis of his business practices, Jeff decided to change how he managed his company—and himself.

Jeff instituted two significant changes at his company. First, he delegated more of the day-to-day responsibilities of running the business to one of his six employees. This put one layer of management between himself and production.

Second, Jeff decided to be less of a manager and more of a leader. He developed long-range goals and gradually took charge of scheduling production, so that he was able to spend more time planning than playing catch-up. For himself, he discovered simple ways he could take time off without feeling guilty. Currently, some of his favorite activities to unwind are: taking longer lunches on beautiful days, playing computer games ten to fifteen minutes each day, and learning to play the guitar.

If Jeff's situation sounds familiar, consider some of the following ways to reduce stress.

Reshape Your Attitude

Recently, I saw a bumper sticker that said, "Attitude is everything." I agree: Attitude is the most essential component of making positive change. Your attitude is always noticed by others, who react accordingly. You may not have control over time, orders, customer demands, or your teenage son, but you do have control over your own attitude. A positive one is simply more productive and more fun. Sometimes, a simple change in attitude makes all the difference.

Delegate Work to Others

One of the common mistakes of owners who are growing their businesses is keeping too much control. After all, they got where they are by doing it all. But often, they don't know when to stop working: 60 to 80 hours per week are commonplace. However, there is a time in all businesses when doing too much yourself is detrimental to you and your business. Know when to delegate tasks, decisions, and responsibility to others on your staff, or when to hire outside help. This frees you to spend more time doing what you intend to do best—building a profitable business.

Stress-Reducing Activities

● *Take up a hobby.* Take up tap-dancing, gardening, volleyball. Many business owners say there aren't enough hours in the day to do their business tasks, let alone spend time on a hobby. However, a hobby can provide new focus, fun, and relaxation. Doing something you enjoy is one of the best stress reducers.

● *Take mini-breaks during the work day.* Take a power nap, read a book, walk around the block, or sit silently for ten minutes, doing nothing. Schedule time each day to do something for yourself that is unrelated to business.

● *Schedule a vacation.* Pick a traditionally slow time of year in your business. Plan a vacation to a place that you find relaxing. Buy nonrefundable airline tickets so you won't be tempted to cancel at the last minute. Many business "emergencies" can be handled by someone other than you. Also, resist the temptation to take your cell phone and fax machine on vacation with you. Leave your business at home.

When you feel stressed or it's summer and you have "beach" fever, wouldn't you love to have some unscheduled fun? Well, you can! Sometimes taking time out from work spontaneously is just what the doctor ordered!

Here are three ways to take a break without worrying about breaking the bank or losing billable hours:

1. Often an appointment gets rescheduled, a project gets postponed a day, or any number of changes to your schedule. Take advantage of these few unscheduled hours. Go for a walk, have lunch with a friend, take a power nap, meditate, see a movie, read a chapter in that book you can never get to, or do anything that is fun for you.

2. If you have a client or colleague to thank for giving you or sending you business, why not ask them to join you in doing something that you love to do but reserve for time off? If you like to sail, take them sailing. If you like to hike, take them on one of your favorite hikes. The possibilities are limitless.

3. If a meeting is postponed and you suddenly have a morning or afternoon free, take advantage by sleeping in late, or picking up your children from camp or day care early and having some family quality time.

25 *"When you have a little spontaneous fun you will be surprised how much better your time management, delegation, inspiration, and business become."*

Don't fall into the trap of filling the unexpected free time with checking e-mail or some other business activity. Give it a try. When you have a little spontaneous fun you will be surprised how much better your time management, delegation, inspiration, and business become.

Look carefully at yourself and your business, and take heed from Jeff's experience. Find ways to put excitement, healthy challenge, and fun back into your business life. Learn to recognize when your stress level is too high. Take two of the above suggestions, and listen to your business coach.

How Do You Spell Success?

WHAT MAKES A BUSINESS SUCCESSFUL? Who decides that it is successful? How do you define success? What measures do you use to determine success?

It is a good idea to look into this before you judge how successful you are. Success includes intrinsic satisfaction, as well as financial rewards.

Looking Back

Whether you're just starting out in business or have been in business for years, it's a good idea to take stock and acknowledge yourself at least once a year in terms of what you think makes you and your business successful.

Try this exercise:

Looking back over the year so far, what goals have you met that make you feel successful?

_____

_____

_____

Write down three goals, then examine each and write about what you did to accomplish each. Ask yourself questions such as:

"What new ideas did I implement, and which ones haven't I implemented yet?"

"What's stopping me?"

"What worked really well this year?"

"What values drive my business?"

"How can I expand upon my strengths and successes?"

"What are the objectives and benchmarks I put in place to accomplish my goals?"

"What made me laugh?"

"Why am I in this business?"

"What project was the most exciting and fun?"

Looking Forward

However, sometimes it's easier to define success not by looking back, but by looking ahead at what you want to accomplish and determining possible success factors.

26 "Sometimes it's easier to define success not by looking back, but by looking ahead at what you want to accomplish."

Try this Exercise:

Imagine that it is December 31st of this year, and you are throwing a party to celebrate your success. Brainstorm three accomplishments you would like to be celebrating. Imagine walking up to the microphone to acknowledge your successes. You might say, "I'm proud to announce the publishing of my book." Or, "We successfully completed the roll-out of our new product line in August! Sales have already surpassed our projections." Or, "I doubled my conference keynote speaking engagements this year." Which of your dream accomplishments do you want to aim for? Imagination is the beginning of possibility. Every great accomplishment starts with an idea or a thought. Sometimes the wildest ideas can lead to a breakthrough in your business.

Next Steps

• Look at all areas of your business. Which areas do you want to focus on to achieve your goals? Marketing and sales? Operations? Financials? R&D? Human Resources?

• Choose one or two areas, and write objectives for achieving your goal(s) in that area. A good objective needs to be specific, measurable, realistic, and set in time. For example, an objective for a catalogue business might be: "Ship 98 percent of orders the same day and 100 percent of orders within three days, consistently, by November 30th." This objective can be graphed and will show you, on a weekly basis, how close to your goal you are. If you see that you are falling behind, you can troubleshoot, make appropriate changes, and move forward.

• Create objectives for achieving your goals that can be measured, and then check your results monthly throughout the year.

• Don't forget to consider personal goals as well. As a business owner, it is very easy to work long hours and let go of leisure activities, hobbies, family time, or community service.

• Look at what you like to do besides business, and make room and time for these activities in your schedule. For example, commit to working 50 hours per week and playing on three out of four weekends; or commit to reading one fiction book a month; or commit to mentoring a young person in your community who is interested in learning about business.

Now that you have re-evaluated and recommitted, what daily success actions will you take? Here are some suggestions:

1. What is the most important task for you to accomplish today?

2. What is the single daily action that will consistently move you toward your business objectives?

3. What is one task you still do that you could turn over to someone who could do it better than you? When you are a solo business owner, you are not good at all tasks. Give up the one task in which you are not as skilled and your business can be more efficient.

4. What one new marketing strategy would be a great referral or word-of-mouth business builder?

5. Are you following up with potential clients within 24 to 48 hours after having a conversation with them?

6. Who already targets the same market as you do? Make a date to discuss a possible collaboration.

7. What is one new action you can take to make things easier for your clients?

How do you spell SUCCESS? Here is one way:

S = Sell by building relationships and offering solutions to customers' needs.

U = Understand your market and find your unique niche.

C = Create value.

C = Control the sails of your business ship, not the wind.

E = Expect success.

S = Support your efforts by asking for help when you need it and giving it when asked.

S = Start small and think big.

Now take a moment and spell success for yourself.

A Fork in the Road:
Which Way Do You Go?

IT'S APRIL. Your taxes are done. You have a clear picture of how well your business did in the previous year.

So, what's next? Are you planning to continue going in the same direction? Or do you change what you've been doing or add a new service or product? This could be a good time to tweak your business plan for the third quarter of the year. In order to grow your business, it's important to invest your time, money, and energy where it will do the most good.

Adding a new service or product, hiring a new employee, or changing your marketing mix can seem overwhelming at first. Change requires making some hard decisions. When you reach your initial growth goals for your business, it's time to move to the next level. This can be daunting for the solo operator: "What if I make the wrong decision?" "How do I research the market?" "How confident am I about making this change?" "Do I have the time and energy to learn quickly what I need to know to make my new venture successful?" But there are ways not to get overwhelmed. Remember, don't be a lone wolf. Get some help. Talk to someone about the fears you have regarding expanding your business. Somehow, when you share your fears with others, they become lighter and more manageable.

27 *"Adding a new service or product, hiring a new employee, or changing your marketing mix can seem overwhelming at first. Change requires making some hard decisions."*

For example, one of my clients is a real estate investor. He wants to diversify his real estate holdings, but he is not sure how to do it. If he sells one of his apartment buildings, he will incur heavy taxes unless he reinvests the proceeds in a similar type of investment, but his dilemma is that he doesn't want to buy another apartment building. What type of commercial property might he consider that will require less intensive on-site management responsibilities and will afford a reasonable rate of return on his investment? I suggested that he might find this problem less daunting and easier to deal with if he looked at it like a project. Then I gave him a simple plan and asked him to check back with me in a few weeks.

At the end of two weeks, he called to tell me that he had decided to purchase a 45-unit building in another state with a solid expanding rental market. I was surprised, because he had been so sure that he didn't want another apartment building. However, his research convinced him that it would work out, because he could hire a property-management company to deal with the day-to-day, on-site management. He discovered that he needed to diversify in terms of location, rather than type of property. He is now ready to sell one building and buy another larger one in a different state.

Treat the Change Like a Project

If you are at a crossroads in your business, it will be easier if you treat the change like a project. Follow these simple rules to make the change happen.

1. *Know what you want to do.* Carefully research the change you are considering. What will it take to make the change? Will you need to hire a new employee? Can you partner with a colleague? Is there really a market for what you want to do? Make a decision based on your research.

2. *Plan what you're going to do.* Develop a plan to implement your new service, product, or process. Set benchmarks to check your progress, including a cutoff date for canceling the project if it proves not to be feasible.

3. *Do what you have to do.* Follow through on your plans. Make adjustments as needed. Get input from other people in your field, or a business consultant, if appropriate. Fold this project into your other responsibilities. Don't lose sight of the services/products you are already offering. Be realistic about the length of time it will take to complete this new project.

4. *Document what you did.* Keep written notes of your progress. Note what worked well and what didn't. Determine the pitfalls of your new venture. Keep a "good ideas" file to capture ideas that come up and that you might want to try later. Use your documentation to evaluate the viability of taking the necessary next steps in your plan.

5. *Evaluate and make appropriate changes.* Now that you've done your research, tested the market, and followed your plan, it's time to decide whether you are going to implement your new idea or not. You have solid information on which to base an intelligent decision. If you decide

to go for it, make any necessary changes and move forward. If you decide not to do it, you have learned a great deal and discovered new ideas that you may want to try at a later date. Next time you are at a crossroads, you'll have a better idea of what to do to grow your business successfully.

CHAPTER 5

MARKET AND SELL YOUR SOCKS OFF!

Mind Your Ps and Qs

AS A KID, my Mom used to tell me to "mind my Ps and Qs." I never quite knew what the Ps and the Qs meant, but I knew they were important in getting along with others and being successful. I've noticed that people who have been in business for awhile mention remarkably similar characteristics that have helped them keep their business and enthusiasm high. Here then, is a list of Ps and Qs that you may consider minding to help maintain and grow your business.

The Ps

Planning.   Planning is essential. For example, write a marketing plan and update it regularly. However, planning is what most people put off. They say, "I'll get to that. Right now, I have my plan in my head." Poor planning is one of the most common reasons for business failure, so take the time to write your objectives, make a plan to meet them, and follow through daily, weekly, and monthly. Track what worked and what didn't, and revise accordingly. Follow the trends that affect your business on a regular basis, and make changes as needed. Pat yourself on the back when business is rolling in; but keep your eye on the future and plan for it. Careful and consistent planning works.

Persistence.   Remember the story of the tortoise and the hare? Who won the race? Keep going. Keep connecting with carefully targeted customers, following up on leads, producing excellent service, and developing ongoing business referrals. However, sometimes you don't need to do anything except listen to

28 "People want to do business with people they can count on to do the job and who will still be in business in ten years."

your customers and continue giving them what they want. In time, your efforts will pay off, just as the tortoise won the race. People want to do business with people they can count on to do the job and who will still be in business in ten years.

Patience. Be like a cat that is after a mouse. Wait until the time is right and then pounce—on opportunities, that is, not on customers. You will want to push your business growth curve, and you may get impatient with slow results.

However, try to do what you can control; then, play the waiting game. Put your marketing plan in motion. If advertising is part of your marketing mix, run your ad for at least three months. Don't pull it too soon. Potential customers may have seen your advertisement nine times before they decide to call you. But then, when they look for your advertisement the next time and it isn't there, they will call someone else. You never know for sure when your prospective customers will sign up for your service or buy your product. Most importantly, be patient with yourself. You can't do it all, or not all at once!

If I had to name one characteristic that is absent from most unsuccessful business people, it would be patience. I take a long-term view of my marketing activities and my business growth. I'm in it for the duration; it's the same way I approach financial investing. Patience will produce consistent results and steady growth. One final thought would be to spend less time pursuing dollars and more time pursuing relationships. Business success is about relationships—and relationships take time.

—**Jeff Rubin,** The Newsletter Guy, Pinole, California

The Qs

Quotas. Sales professionals have sales quotas. So should you. Figure out what you need to make this year in order to turn a profit. Set sales benchmarks for your company. Break down your projected sales for the year into monthly sales quotas. Keep track of the sources that produce the most income. Adjust your work to focus more time and effort on those sources in order to build business and increase cash flow. Make time for those activities that may not generate immediate income but will generate ongoing business.

Developing and maintaining your own professional network will keep you up-to-date on market trends, produce referrals, and create valuable business connections.

Quality. When was the last time you experienced excellent customer service? Quality is easily recognized, but can be a challenge to produce. Too often, companies extol their superior customer service, but don't follow through. If you consistently provide excellent service, your business will thrive. People will drive miles to do business with you. Customers want products that work, service that gives them value, and responsive, polite, effective customer service when problems arise. If customers are unhappy with your service, resolve it; don't give them a laundry list of excuses. We're a service-oriented economy. Your type of business can be duplicated by many others. You will stand out by delivering quality service and being responsive to your customers.

Quiet Time. Allow yourself free time to do those things you like to do but think you can't because you have too much to do for your business. Your business will improve if you take quiet time for yourself. Of course, this doesn't mean that you have to meditate. Your quiet time could be the simple pleasure of reading a good book or walking on a beach. Whatever gives you a sense of peace and quiet, build it into your weekly schedule. Some business owners say that taking regular vacations helps their business grow. Why do you think that is so? It allows you time to relax, and gives you a new perspective on handling your business with renewed energy.

Why Market Research?

REMEMBER THE LINE from the movie, *Field of Dreams*, "Build it and they will come"? Many first-time owners simply open the doors of their business and expect that customers will rush in to buy their new widget or service. On rare occasions, this is exactly what happens. However, for most new businesses, it takes careful planning and positioning to bring in customers and keep them. Your business will not succeed just because you are enthusiastic about your product and you want to succeed. This will provide the motivation to build your business, but the business must be built on careful initial and ongoing planning.

Is There a Market?

The first step is to determine whether there actually is a market for your products or services. This process is called market research. Analyzing your market and competition will help you decide whether to open your business doors. However, before you do extensive and expensive market research, ask yourself and other people in your field these questions:

- How many competitors provide the same service or product?

- If your product or service is innovative (i.e., not already known to the public), can you educate your market and create a demand for it?

- Can you compete effectively in price, quality, and delivery?

- Can you price your product or service to achieve a profit?

Researching the Market

If you feel satisfied that you do have a viable idea, move to the next step of researching your market in the areas of target customers, competitors, and industry trends:

- *Target Customers*: Who are they? Where are they? How many are there? Is your service essential in their day-to-day activity? What are their needs and resources? Can they afford your products?

- *Competitors*: Who are they? How many are there? Where are they? How is their business similar or different from yours? What are their pricing strategies, what are their value-added services?

- *Industry Trends*: What is declining or growing in the industry as a whole or locally? What's happening in the general economy that might affect the buying trends of your customers? Is the industry seasonal?

This research effort pays off in increased profit potential, because you gain solid data that helps you to:

- Find out if there is enough demand for your product or service.

- Determine the promotional mix that's most likely to reach your target customers.

- Develop critical short- and mid-term goals.

- Identify and prepare for market changes.

Defining Your Market Niche

After your market research is complete, it's time to ask yourself the question: "*Why will customers buy from me?*" The answer is your competitive advantage. You must determine this before you promote your business. When you define your market niche clearly, you will spend your time, money, and effort in satisfying customers who value your niche. For example, you may want your business to be the women's clothing boutique that features the latest fashions from New York or Paris. Spend your time and dollars on becoming known for what differentiates your business from your competition.

29 *"After your market research is complete, it's time to ask yourself the question: "Why will customers buy from me?" The answer is your competitive advantage."*

Market research is essential to help you develop your niche. A market niche does not just happen. It is carefully thought out and planned. Yet once you clearly have a market niche, the right customers find your door and will come again and again.

If you have read this far and are thinking of starting a business, you may be thinking, "This is a lot of work. Can't I just make my best guess and see how it goes?" Yes, you can. Just remember that well over 50 percent of businesses fail in the first five years of business. And one of the biggest reasons is poor planning. If you do your market research at the beginning and track market changes on a regular basis (every six months to a year, depending on your industry), yours will be one of the businesses that SUCCEED.

A Quick and Easy Competition Study

To help you better position your business, check out your competition. *Remember*: Your competitors can include educators, friends, and foes. All types can provide useful information. You simply use different techniques to gather information, depending on the type of competition. Talk to your competitors, ask questions, do informational interviews with those who are willing, act like a customer yourself, or send a mystery shopper.

In the following exercise, choose at least two elements and compare how your business or business idea deals with them in contrast to how at least two of your competitors deal with them.

1. Pricing

2. Delivery

3. Hours available

4. Location

5. Promotion

6. Quality

7. Web presence

8. Selection of services

9. "Value-added" offerings

10. Other: _____

My Business	*Competitor 1*	*Competitor 2*
_____	_____	_____
_____	_____	_____
_____	_____	_____
_____	_____	_____

Going Green and Saving the Environment

What Is a Green Business?

Since the release of Al Gore's movie, *An Incovenient Truth*, there has been a national and international upsurge in concern for global warming and saving our earth. It has filtered down into all types of businesses, large and small, in the form of creating a healthy work environment and being environmentally conscious in communities and the world, proactively.

You can find a lot of information on the Internet through federal, local, and county governments and through nonprofit organizations about how to make your business more "green" or environmentally conscious. In my research, I discovered that the Green Business Program (greenbiz.ca.gov) in California has a model program that is being emulated in other parts of the United States. Their requirements for certifying companies as "green" comply with the national standards set by the United States Environmental Protection Agency (epa.gov).

All types and sizes of businesses qualify to "go green." For example, auto repair shops, printers, hotels, restaurants, landscapers, wineries, janitorial and laundry services, grocery and retail stores, builders, attorneys, architects, engineers, gift services, business consultants, and a variety of office and home-based businesses can apply and can successfully meet the standards.

Yet, much like organic farmers, you might choose to have a green business without being officially certified green by your county government. At my local farmers market, many of the stalls have signs that say "organically grown without pesticides." Ask yourself what you can do in your home office or place of business that helps the environment generally and creates a healthy workplace for you and your employees.

Can you:

* Comply with or exceed all applicable environmental regulations for your business?

* Conserve energy, water, materials, and other resources?

* Develop and implement practices that prevent pollution and waste, such as recycling, carpooling, or bicycling to work?

Why Get Certified As a Green Business?

Getting certified as a green business makes good business sense, both for the bottom line and the environment. With all the concern about global warming, people everywhere are motivated to do their part in reducing their carbon footprint. Many people become loyal customers of companies who are certified as "green," and this can give companies a marketing edge. Some other advantages are:

30 *"Getting certified as a green business makes good business sense, both for the bottom line and the environment."*

* Employees appreciate working in a healthy environment.

* Operating efficiently can strengthen the bottom line.

* Green companies can gain recognition as environmental leaders. In California, for example, Acterra: Action for a Sustainable Earth gives annual Business Environmental Awards to companies that demonstrate that they are successful in three ways—economically, environmentally, and socially—by integrating exemplary sustainability practices into their daily business operations.

- Many customers prefer to shop locally at small businesses to support their local economy and to save on gas and air pollution.

More and more it is true that becoming a green small business is an added marketing advantage!

Real Entrepreneurs Going Green

About two years ago, a mortgage broker in my business networking group announced proudly that she had become certified as a green business. Because I didn't really know what that meant at the time, I asked her to explain it to me. Jenny Shore runs a small branch office for Alternative Mortgage, an independent mortgage brokerage firm. She said that she contacted her local county Green Business program and arranged for her business to be evaluated. Much to her surprise, Jenny discovered that she had already been doing some of the "green" compliance recommendations, such as recycling, reducing the use of paper, and bicycling to work.

In order to become a certified Green Business, there is a specific process required by every local county agency that typically involves inspections by the local electric and gas company and waste management company. Specific recommendations are then made to each business on how to reduce waste and use of paper resources.

Jenny is also a founding member of the Build It Green Real Estate Council. One business advantage that Jenny has noticed is that many potential clients call her because of her knowledge of green mortgages and green real estate in general. A *green mortgage* is essentially a mortgage that rewards the homeowner for reducing waste, reducing energy usage, and building with environmentally responsible materials. Even if a client isn't looking for a green mortgage, most clients are pleased that Jenny is a green business and make a point of commenting on it. Jenny says, "I'm proud of my green focus and I'm sure my passion for helping my clients reduce their environmental impact plays a role in the growth of my business."

As a Berkeley caterer, Hugh Groman, says:

It's a win-win-win situation. My business, my clients, and the environment all benefit from my company's efforts to run an environmentally conscious company. Everyone cares about the environment now. It's a smart business decision because more and more people want to do business with "green" businesses. It's a marketing edge.

For his catering company, Hugh uses low-flow water sprayers and LED lightbulbs; saves cooking oil, which can be used for bio-diesel; uses compostable disposable plates, cups, and silverware; recycles whenever possible; composts all food and other organic waste at the kitchen and at his off-site events; and uses e-mail for all catering proposals and communication. In addition, Hugh's website is his brochure, and he uses generic business cards for all employees so they don't waste cards each time there is a change.

When I interviewed Catherine Smith, president of World Class Charters, Inc., she was very excited about finding a way for her company to "go green." Catherine charters corporate jets to Fortune 500 corporations and high-wealth individuals for private flights. Catherine shared that she recently talked with The Conservation Fund in order to begin implementing their Go CarbonZero Program, which will plant trees to offset carbon emissions of private jet flights arranged by her company. The Go CarbonZero Program will calculate the emissions by type of jet, number of hours flown, and fuel burned to determine how much the donation should be for each flight.

Most of Catherine's customers are well-educated industry executives who she is sure will welcome the opportunity to exhibit social responsibility while still conducting their business in a time-efficient manner. Catherine says, "I'm proud to say that World Class Charters will be the first private aviation charter company offering their customers the ability to offset carbon emissions associated with air travel." For more information about the Go CarbonZero Program, visit conservationfund.org and gocarbonzero.org.

How Can My Business Get Certified?

For your business, the best way to find out how you can go green in your community and what specific practices you can implement, is to contact your county government and local small business trade associations. In California, you can contact the Green Business Program (greenbiz.ca.gov). If there is no program in your community, you can participate in national programs most notably the EPA's Performance Track program. (epa.gov/performancetrack).

Other resources for going green are:

- *Energy Star* (energystar.gov) is a joint program of the U.S. Environmental Protection Agency and the U.S. Department of Energy, which helps individuals and businesses save money and protect the environment through efficient products and services. It offers energy management strategies for businesses that help businesses measure current energy performance, set goals, track savings, and reward improvement.

- *Enviroene* (es.epa.gov) attempts to provide a single repository for pollution prevention, compliance assurance and enforcement, and information and resources on how you can reduce air pollution in your daily life and your business.

- *CoopAmerica* (coopamerica.org) is a national nonprofit membership organization, whose mission is "to harness the power—the strength of consumers, investors, and businesses—to create a socially just and environmentally friendly sustainable society." They produce Green Festivals and many resources for individuals and businesses.

Six Secrets of Marketing Your Business

AT THE END OF THE YEAR, look back over what you have accomplished in your business and ask yourself: "What made my business successful? What marketing techniques brought in the best results? What flopped? What do I need to do differently or better next year?"

When you're redoing your marketing plan for the next year, keep these six "secrets" in mind:

31 "A marketing plan does no good collecting dust on a shelf. Implement and measure each marketing activity. See what works and what doesn't."

1. *Write and work your marketing plan.* A plan does no good collecting dust on a shelf. Implement and measure each marketing activity. See what works and what doesn't. Make appropriate changes based on client response.

2. *Be visible as an expert in your field.* Speak at professional organizations, conferences, and clubs. Write articles for industry newsletters, local newspapers, and magazines. Start your own e-newsletter or write a book.

3. *Follow up.* Always do what you promise and, when possible, do more than is expected. You will create loyal customers and great word-of-mouth referrals.

4. *Choose marketing techniques appropriate for your target market(s) and use them consistently.* One mistake entrepreneurs make is using techniques with which they are comfortable, but which don't effectively reach their market.

5. *Build, maintain, and nurture a network of contacts and colleagues.* Don't be a lone wolf. Few business owners have built their business without help. A network of contacts and colleagues is the most important for building a successful business, especially for sole proprietors. It is a source of support, guidance, strategic alliances, and marketing ideas, as well as referrals.

6. *Get free publicity.* But how? Consider some of these practical publicity tips from an expert, Patrick Galvin of Galvin Communications in Portland, Oregon:

   * *Play up what is different and unusual.* Pay attention to what everyone else in your niche is doing and do something else to get noticed.

   * *Find a timely news hook.* Reporters are looking for stories that feed into current events and reflect larger, socioeconomic trends.

   * *Localize a national story or trend.* Journalists are always looking for ways to illustrate a national story or trend with local examples.

   * *Appeal to emotion.* Use visual elements, humor, or drama to stand apart. Be careful not to go overboard.

   * *Provide news that you can use.* The media is fascinated with giving their audience news that it can put to practical use. "How to" articles and "tips and techniques" are perennial public relations favorites.

   * *Keep it simple.* Journalists are looking for stories that are easily digestible and not overly complicated. Focus on one aspect of the big picture instead of the big picture itself.

To further illustrate the above points, Patrick Galvin says, "Consider your own business expertise. How can you translate what you know into a press release offering people news they can use? For instance, if you're a chiropractor, what tips can you offer so people don't injure their backs? Surely your experience with back injury patients has given you valuable insight into how people get injured and how these injuries can be avoided. Your local newspaper might be interested in this information, especially if you provide tips that people haven't seen before. And if you are aiming for television coverage, offer ideas for interesting ways to present the information visually."

Remember: Don't try to do too much at once. By carrying out just one or two of the marketing secrets above, you can create a wonderfully successful business.

Marketing = Sales!

AS YOU CAN SEE, everything you do is marketing—from answering the phone to placing an ad. And marketing leads to sales.

It's very important to choose your marketing strategies carefully. Make sure you diversify your marketing portfolio. Choose from the tips in many areas so you reach as much of your target market in as many ways through as much media as you can.

Mix up some ads, some website, some direct mail, some publicity and networking to start. Why do this? To reach as much of your target market as possible in as many ways as you can—realizing not everyone will see you in every media. Not everyone reads magazines, goes to your website, reads your e-mail, or sees your ads.

Here are the categories from which to select tips to add to your marketing plan. This is not an exhaustive list, but you can add to it as you go along. Put a check mark next to the tips that best fit your marketing plan. Choose at least one from each category:

Networking

_____ Attend at least three meetings of associations to find a good one for you to network with.

_____ Test some formalized leads groups to stimulate sales.

_____ Tell six to ten people about your business each week at business and social events.

_____ Prepare a 30-second elevator speech clearly explaining what you sell and whom it benefits.

_____ Ask potential clients about their business and their needs.

Promotion

_____ Diversify the use of your promotional tools. Include websites, e-commerce, e-bulletin boards, newsgroups, direct mail, fliers, brochures, events, speaking to groups, or advertising to reach your entire target market.

_____ Develop your own opt-in e-mail list. Send out an e-newsletter or Special Report. *Note*: Always have a consistent look, image, and message to make an impact on your market.

Publicity

_____ Write articles to pitch to publications or websites for content.

_____ Select publications or media that are read or viewed by your target market.

_____ Submit an online press release that reflects a current trend or story in the news.

_____ Seek radio interviews local and national if you are an author.

Advertising

_____ Test ads in print and online, targeting exactly the market you seek.

_____ If you have the budget, test only Pay Per Click, TV, or radio commercials to reach your target market at prime hours of the day.

_____ Write compelling copy that sells the solution to your market's problem in an enticing way.

_____ Place a call to action in your ads, giving readers an incentive to call your business. *Note*: Always track where callers found your ad so you can evaluate what is working and what is not.

Sales

_____ Create a good impression by talking with and listening to your prospects, either in person or by telephone.

_____ Focus on filling your pipeline, following up, giving presentations, and asking for the business.

_____ Make it easy and convenient to buy your service or products.

Remember, it's the strategy you use, not the tools that ensure your success. Clearly defining your target market, sending a clear message, and staying consistent is key.

32 *"It's the strategy you use, not the tools that ensure your success. Clearly defining your target market, sending a clear message, and staying consistent is key."*

Ten Simple Ways to Get Referrals

HAVE YOU EVER HEARD a consultant proudly say, "I get all my business through referrals"? Have you ever wondered how they accomplished that? Generally speaking, most people want to do business with people they know, like, and trust. People ask friends for referrals, trust their judgment and try out their recommendation. You, as the consultant or small business owner, also get a pre-qualified lead for your business—a person who most likely fits the criteria for your ideal client or customer. "Word of mouth" saves you time and money. The client is primed to buy your product or try out your service, and you haven't spent any advertising dollars.

33 *"*"Word of mouth" saves you time and money. The client is primed to buy your product or try out your service, and you haven't spent any advertising dollars.*"*

Here is an excellent example of following up on a referral:

Mark Estes, a photographer, says that marketing and sales sparks creativity in him. Mark recommends that you ask yourself each day: "What 10 things can I do to promote my business?" It could be six phone calls, three e-mails and one thank you note. Mine your own clients for referrals because they are the ones who know you and appreciate your work.

Mark recently followed up on a referral to a company about presenting his portfolio to let them know what he had to offer. He received an immediate e-mail in return, which said, "Funny you should call today. Just this morning, we discovered that we need our annual report done earlier then expected. Can you help us with the photography?" Mark suggested that the manager look at his portfolio on his website and find an image that could be applicable to their project. He did and Mark went that week to do the photo shoot. Mark says even if you don't get a meeting with the current referral, keep asking one more question, such as, "Do you know any publishers who might need head shots for authors?"

Perhaps you are saying to yourself, "I've heard this before. I know I should be marketing my business more, but I can't seem to get started." So here are 10 simple ways to create referrals:

1. Tell six to ten people about your business each week. Don't leave your office without your business cards and your 30-second answer to the question, "What do you do?"

2. Project a consistent image of your company in all promotional materials—business cards, letterhead, postcards, website, newsletters, and advertisements.

3. Be client-driven: Meet their needs. The number-one way to find out what clients want is to ask—and then listen. Respond by acknowledging their request and developing a solution. Then deliver consistently and on time.

4. In initial customer contacts, be welcoming and willing to answer questions or concerns. On voicemail, leave an informative message and let clients know when they can reach you and when you'll get back to them; then, follow through. Good first impressions are crucial.

5. Consider a double-sided business card. Put a menu of services and products on the flipside. It serves as a mini-brochure.

6. Keep a calendar of your marketing activities for each month. Attend at least two activities per month, even when you're busy! This keeps potential customers in the pipeline. Revise your calendar according to what type of marketing activities work the best for your business. Add more of the activities that work, and drop the ones that don't.

7. Join and participate actively in your local Chamber of Commerce and appropriate professional organizations and community groups. Remember, people do business with people they know and like.

8. Practice the art of conversation—listening and sharing, and getting to know more about your customer or potential client. Conversation is a give-and-take proposition, like a dance. Be friendly, humorous, engaging, and not just focused on doing business. People will appreciate you and your interest in them.

9. Walk your talk. How can you advise people to do what you yourself are not doing? Do what you advise others to do, and make sure you deliver.

10. Set aside time every day to do one marketing activity—even if it's a five-minute telephone call. This will constantly keep you connected with your current and potential customers. People can't do business with you if they don't know who you are or what you have to offer.

And here is a bonus tip:

11. Add to this list. Choose just one idea and use it consistently for a month.

The Number One Key to successful marketing is to choose a set of simple and effective marketing activities that match your strategic plan, and do them consistently.

The Number Two Key is to choose those activities that best fit your target market(s), rather than what is easy for you to do. Most importantly, remember that the most carefully detailed marketing plan on paper won't work unless you make it real by putting it into action.

Six Sales Tips to Help You Sell with Confidence

YOUR BUSINESS PLAN IS DONE. Your office is in order. Your business cards, brochure, website, and ads are ready. You even have a list of qualified leads. There's only one thing left to do is, and it scares you silly—sell! How can you take the scariness out of sales? Turn those customers into friendly folks who need solutions to very real problems. Think of yourself as a problem buster.

Tip 1: Listen

Your potential customers want something. That's why they're calling you in the first place. It does little good to tell them about all your services when they may only be interested in one. Find out what that is by asking questions and listening to the answers. If you have a service that you truly think will help this customer, explain it to them. Ask if they have any questions or need further information or clarification. Often your customer may simply appreciate that you listened to them. If they don't buy then, they'll remember you, and they'll either buy later or refer your service to others. Don't forget to follow up with them at regular intervals.

Listen to your client's expectations. Know yourself and what you can deliver. I had years of social work behind me when I started my business. This was invaluable in knowing how to handle people with respect. I think humility is a tremendous asset. Be willing to listen to your client to see if you're giving her what she wants. Learn from your mistakes and apologize when you're wrong. You will carry the day and make any situation redeemable. Don't take anything personally or let your ego get involved.

—**Pauline Pearsall,** Pauline Pearsall Staging, Oakland, California

Tip 2: Share

Think of selling as sharing information, resources, and helpful suggestions. The personal touch of calling, rather than sending written information by fax, e-mail, or snail mail, makes a big difference. Smile, call customers by name, and avoid being pushy. Deliver your product on time, and follow up. When people decide to buy something, they usually feel a sense of urgency. Make sure you do what you promised as well as delivering a quality product or service. This builds trust and return business.

Tip 3: Qualify Your Customers

You can follow the first two tips to the letter, but if you're talking to people who don't want or can't afford your product, you're wasting your efforts. For example, no matter how wonderful your cold-water taffy is, a person with dentures won't bite. Make sure you are reaching the appropriate target market for your business.

Tip 4: Offer Solutions

Match your service or product to the customer's needs. If there is not an exact match, you may actually offer the best-fitting solution, which customers can try on their own. Then you say, "If that doesn't work out for you, call me and I'll be happy to help you." Also, don't talk about the features of your product or service before the customer has bought into its benefits. Ask powerful questions that are open-ended; this helps your customers clarify their needs. When a customer is very interested in your service but is not ready to move forward, ask, "What would have to happen for you to make a decision?" Her answer will allow you to offer a more specific solution that matches her needs.

34 *"How can you take the scariness out of sales? Turn those customers into friendly folks who need solutions to very real problems."*

Tip 5: Build Relationships

Be visible in your community. Participate in trade, professional, and social organizations. Most national professional organizations have chapters in major cities. Offer to give a talk at one of these organizations in your area. They are always looking for good speakers. You are not the only salesperson for your company; customers who like what you have to offer will refer their friends to you. People want to do business with people they know. It has been shown that satisfied customers tell three people about the product or service they liked. If you have 50 actual customers, this means you have 150 potential customers. Be the merchant in your community who's known for friendly, reliable service, or the consultant who is happy to refer a colleague if her expertise doesn't fit a customer's needs.

Tip 6: Ask Powerful Questions

Powerful questions are questions that are open-ended and allow for your clients or prospects to give you more information or insight into who they are, and what their needs and concerns are. Some examples of powerful questions are:

"Tell me more about your project."

"What has been working so far?"

"What seems to be missing?"

"How have you been dealing with this difficult issue?"

"What would it take for you to be willing to try out our product?"

Powerful questions are much more effective than questions that elicit simple Yes or No answers.

There are many ways to make life easier for your customers, such as answering their requests promptly, solving a problem the same day, taking the time to chat, or offering free delivery. Most people have too many daily hassles to deal with, so you can make doing business with you a bright spot in their day.

How to Get Unstuck in the Sales Cycle

THERE ARE FOUR basic stages in the sales cycle:

1. Create a customer list to fill your sales pipeline.

2. Follow up, follow up, and follow up!

3. Get a meeting or present your portfolio.

4. Close the sale!

If you're not closing as many sales as you would like it's time to analyze where in the sales cycle you are stuck. Answer the questions in the following exercise. Be honest yet gentle with yourself:

 "If you're not closing as many sales as you would like it's time to analyze where in the sales cycle you are stuck."

In which stage am I stuck? Why?

_____

What might I need to do differently about the way I've been selling?

_____

What tools, information, techniques, ideas, or skills do I need to build a customer list to fill the pipeline, follow up, get presentations, or close sales?

_____

Key: Each stage will probably need different tools and skills.

Narrow your focus to one stage. For example, you may be filling the pipeline, but you are ignoring the follow up. Or you are getting meetings but not closing sales.

List three actions you plan to take to get moving in the area you are stuck:

1. _____

2. _____

3. _____

Focus on this one stage and these actions. Work your plan consistently for one month.

Fear might get in your way. Just remember what FEAR actually means:

False **E**vidence **A**ppearing **R**eal

Build in support from your colleagues, ask for advice from your coach, or read books that help you with actions to take to get you moving forward. Do whatever works for you to get unstuck!

Position Yourself to Sell a Solution

NO MATTER WHAT BUSINESS you are in, you are selling something. Why will people buy from you? It's because you have something they want, or they have something to gain by doing business with you. People want to buy solutions to problems. No matter what you sell, you have competitors. So what compels people to choose you? Two things: uniqueness and benefits.

Uniqueness

What makes your business unique? Determine your business's uniqueness by asking yourself questions such as:

- "What do customers praise most when they e-mail, write, or talk to us?"
- "How do employees, customers, suppliers, and friends describe what we do?"

- "What do we offer that our competitors can't?"

- "What problems do our product or service solve?"

- "If my mother-in-law were buying a service like ours, what would she look for?"

Then ask your customers questions like these:

- "How would you describe our product to your friends?"

- "What would you say to recommend our service?"

- "What made you choose our service?"

- "What do we do that you haven't found at other similar companies?"

- "How can we improve our service or product line?"

- "Why do you visit our store/place of business often?"

As you compile and ponder this information and do some ongoing market research, it will become clearer to you what makes your business unique. Position your marketing to deliver that message—a message that answers the customer's basic question, "What's in it for me?" Get very specific so that people who hear or read about what you offer will know what problem you will solve and the benefits of doing business with you.

When you have decided what makes your business unique, make up a catchy slogan of four to nine words that paints a picture of your business. For example, an accountant might say, "We do numbers right!" Be creative; add a dash of humor. Describe in a few words what differentiates you from your competitors in terms of size, customer-service policies, employees, mission, speed, cost, or time. This "picture" of your business makes it easy for current customers to refer you to others.

Benefits

Whatever you are selling, benefits are what your customers are buying. What benefits do your customers get from you? Business owners often make the mistake of selling features rather than benefits. In a market where many companies sell similar products or services, the customer wants to know what benefits you offer.

For example, when you buy a car you know that all cars will provide you with transportation. However, you select a particular car because of its benefits, such as one that fits your budget, your climate, and your self-image. Here are a few more examples of the difference between selling features and benefits:

Feature	Benefit
24-hour grocery store	It allows you to buy food at your convenience.
Airbags	It protects you and passengers in case of an accident.
Accounting services	It helps you sleep better, knowing that your books balance.

Which benefits are your customers buying? Often the most direct way to find out is simply to ask them. You may think you are offering certain benefits, but do your customers think so as well? Find out by giving them a simple questionnaire and asking them these questions:

1. List what you like about our product or service.

2. What is the single most important reason you buy our product or service?

3. What convinced you to buy our product or service instead of a competing one?

36 *"Because others have similar products/services to yours, your primary product is actually how well and how consistently you reward a customer's confidence in you."*

Then ask these same questions of your best customers and continue asking "What else?" until you uncover the real reason they keep coming back. Build your business around that.

Remember: Because others have similar products/services to yours, your primary product is actually how well and how consistently you reward a customer's confidence in you.

To grow your business, know what makes you unique and what customers perceive as the benefits of doing business with you. And keep delivering those benefits.

Why Customers Should Buy from You

ONCE YOU HAVE DETERMINED your target market(s), you want these potential customers to know about your product or service and why they should buy from you.

Marketing is all the activities you initiate to secure your position within the market, or the total possibilities for generating revenues for your product or service. When you have determined who your target market is and your slice of the total market, it's time to craft your positioning statement—a statement that answers the question: "Why should I buy from you?"

The Importance of the Positioning Statement

Your positioning statement shows how you differ from your competitors; it differentiates your business and emphasizes your uniqueness. A well-crafted statement is a very effective *sales tool*! It is a concise, powerful statement that, when delivered genuinely, will go a long way toward closing a sale. It can also be used to introduce yourself at networking events. It is often called "the 30-second elevator speech," because that is about as much time as someone will listen to you before they start asking questions or move on to the next person. You want to pique their interest, so they want to find out more about how you might help their business.

The positioning statement, or 30-second elevator speech, has three components:

1. Your company and/or your name

2. A statement about how your product/service addresses the problem/need, as identified by your target customer

3. Your key point of differentiation (your niche)

Here are some ways to differentiate your business:

- An impressive list of clients

- A solid customer-service track record

- A unique approach that delivers better results

- Added value to your product or service

- A focus on specific deliverables in quality, service, or price

- A specific target market

Here is an example of an effective 30-second elevator speech:

Hi, I'm Dana Arkinzadeh and my business is DMA Organizing. I am a professional organizer of homes and businesses in Alameda County (California). Interested in improving your health? Clear out your clutter and get organized! Don't lose a contract because you couldn't assemble the information needed to do a proposal! Disorganization causes stress and stress can directly affect your health. Improve your health by letting a professional organizer take the stress out of getting organized! Go from clutter to clarity with DMA Organizing.

How to Make Your 30-Second Elevator Speech Count

It's time to re-evaluate how you are presenting yourself and your business. Research claims that people decide to hire you or do business with you within the first 30 seconds of meeting you. That is why having an effective 30-second elevator speech, or sound bite, is so critical. In fact, it is very important to develop several sound bites that fit your niche and market in order to grab the attention of the speed-of-light folks who get literally hundreds of e-mails daily.

37 *"Research claims that people decide to hire you or do business with you within the first 30 seconds of meeting you."*

If we apply this to you and your small business, it is essential to have one to three great sound bites that let your listeners know how wonderful you are or how unique your product/services are. My business sound bite is: "I save small business owners from writing their own pink slip!"

Here are two formats for writing your own:

1. *Tell a Problem—Solution—Story*: People have a problem and come to you to help them solve it. Get their attention by describing a problem, briefly stating how you solve it, and painting a picture by telling a success story.

2. *Say what you do best*: Give an example that illustrates this. For example:

Marketing Consultant: I get the word out about your business. Last week, a client called to say he got seven inquiries the same day his ad ran in the newspaper!

Give it a try. Start by making a list of specific ideas you want to get across. Next, write one to three sentences using one of the formats above. Read it out loud. Refine and rewrite it. Eliminate extra words that don't add anything. Then, try it out with two to three people, get feedback, and revise it accordingly. You're now ready to try it out. Keep practicing your sound bite(s) until you feel confident and comfortable delivering it.

Try It!

My company and my name are: _____

_____

I/We work with (target customers): _____

_____

They are/have (state problem or need here): _____

_____

Our product/service is: _____

_____

This provides (key benefit): _____

_____

What differentiates my service/product (your niche) in the marketplace is: _____

_____

_____

Strategic Networking

THE BASIC NETWORKING PROCESS is a highly successful marketing strategy for getting you into companies before they actually formally begin looking for a consultant to help them solve a problem. If you happen to show up just when they're thinking they need someone who can do what you offer, your sales process is shortened, and you may be able to sign a contract very quickly. Why? Because (1) you don't have to compete with other consultants, (2) you have a great opportunity to show how your skills can benefit them and provide solutions for their immediate needs, and (3) most companies prefer to hire consultants they know, or who are referred to them by trusted colleagues, friends, and employees.

Networking Tips

- Networking is a valuable skill for many business purposes. Build relationships with your network contacts. Everyone networks, especially when looking for new business or consultants.

- A key building block is a well-prepared two-minute introduction or presentation that clearly and succinctly gets across what you have to offer. Customize your introduction to fit your prospect.

- Pursue leads systematically to obtain more meetings.

- Good follow-up is as important as good meetings. You will get results if you keep following up with your contacts. You will also stand out from the pack. It's amazing how many business people don't return phone calls or e-mails, nor follow up with what they promised.

- Networking definitely leads to business meetings. Well-conducted informal meetings produce door-opening referrals, as well as insight into a particular company's needs and culture.

Here Is a System to Help You Make Networking Pay Off

1. Research your target company(s). Find out as much as possible about the company's culture, products, services, changes, or problems faced, as well as the names of key contacts.

2. Talk to friends and colleagues to find a contact within the company with whom you might be able to meet before you send the approach letter to the key contact.

3. Develop an approach letter. Your goal is a meeting with the key contact. Use a referral name, if you have one—it improves your chance of

getting a meeting dramatically. In the letter, include some information that you gleaned from your research, and include a day and time when you will call.

4. Develop a 15-second phone script and follow up the letter with a call at the time you stated. Request a time for an informal meeting.

5. After you schedule a meeting, plan what you want to cover in the meeting. The meeting outline can include:

   - *A Brief Presentation*: Your two-minute introduction, which captures your experience and strengths and illustrates specifically how you might be able to work together.

   - *Main Discussion:* Be prepared with two or three questions about the company's issues. Keep discussion conversational; acknowledge the other person's ideas, ask follow-up questions.

   - *Generating Referrals*: Ask for referrals, especially if there doesn't seem to be a match between the company's needs and your services. Ask for a specific type of referral.

   - *Handling Referrals*: Ask questions such as: "Why does she come to mind?" "How do you happen to know him?" "In what areas do you think she could be helpful or especially interested in my expertise?" Answers to these questions help you write a better approach letter or make a more effective phone call to the referral. Also, ask if you should call the referral yourself or if the person making the referral would prefer to make the call on your behalf.

   - *Ending the Meeting*: Stick to your time agreement. Take the initiative to end the meeting. If appropriate, ask what the next step would be to move forward with a consulting assignment or joint project. If the person is willing to talk longer, she or he will indicate interest. Express your thanks.

6. Debrief yourself directly after the meeting. Write notes so that you remember the information; jot down questions and everything that the person told you about the company.

7. Follow up the meeting with a thank-you letter or e-mail, whichever is appropriate.

8. Follow up with each referral, using the same procedure.

9. Create a system for keeping track of each referral meeting date, connections, important information gained, and results of each referral meeting.

10. Follow leads and possible projects or contracts as far as you can with the target company(ies).

> Business is first and foremost about people, relationships, and community. Build lasting relationships by helping others build their business. When I join a business networking group, my goal is to help twenty other businesses grow. My experience has been that their businesses and mine have grown way beyond our expectations!
>
> —**Jim Horan,** One Page Business Plan Company, Berkeley, California

38 *"If your initial contact doesn't pan out and you still want to work with a company, keep in touch—it may result in work when you least expect it!"*

Contacts made and relationships built will lead to projects coming your way. If your initial contact doesn't pan out and you still want to work with a company, keep in touch—it may result in work when you least expect it!

Customer Service as a Sales Tool

SEVERAL YEARS AGO, I attended a motivational sales training program at a very successful company. After I gave a talk to about 100 employees, I approached the CEO of the company and said, "I can pick out your top three producers from this audience." The CEO, intrigued, said, "Okay, show me who they are." I pointed to three individuals in the audience. Amazed, the CEO asked, "How did you know? Those three people are consistent producers, even in downtimes."

"Easy," I said. "While I was giving my talk, I looked out at the audience. The three people I picked were obviously engaged and listening to me. But beyond that, I felt an intangible feeling of connection with them—call it interest or enthusiasm. They caught my eye and I felt heard. Your customers feel the same way, and they buy from them."

What does this story have to do with delivering quality customer service? Everything. Building a relationship with your customers grows your business. Listening, professionalism, and your unique way of adding value to your service create customer loyalty.

Here are four ways for small-business owners to deliver excellent customer service:

1. Cultivate the quality of listening demonstrated in the story. Customers are not shy about telling you what they want. Listen, ask questions, and then deliver what they want to the best of your ability. For example, a small bookstore may take a few days longer to receive a book you ordered, but if the owner knows what you like to read, he may make helpful recommendations. As a result, you are more likely to order from him, especially if he calls or sends you a postcard when new books arrive that fit your taste.

2. Be responsive. How many times have you called a business and been put on hold for five minutes or told that you need to speak to someone else who will call you right back and never does? A few simple ways to stand out among your competitors is:

   * Return calls promptly.

   * Fax or e-mail information the same day it is requested.

   * Place an order immediately.

   * Get a written proposal in before the deadline.

   * Have a friendly, detailed, helpful message on your voicemail.

   * Answer calls in person or hire a receptionist.

   * Refer customers to another professional if you don't offer what the customer wants.

   * Do what you promise and be willing to handle problems as they arise.

3. Get to know your customers beyond the scope of business. Be generous with your time, especially when dealing with new customers or clients. Make them feel welcome and comfortable. Build a friendly relationship. Be personable, warm, and genuinely interested in them. For example, my family has gone to the same dentist for years. His office hours and

location aren't very convenient, but we all love going to him because he tells jokes and remembers to ask something about each one of us. How many people go to the dentist and get to laugh?

4. Try to handle the dissatisfied customer diplomatically. Dissatisfied customers are more likely to tell people what they disliked about your service than satisfied customers will tell people what they liked. For example, I bought an outfit from a small boutique, but after getting it home, I decided I didn't like it. The next day, I took it back to the store and asked if I could exchange it or get store credit. Since it was on sale, the clerk told me that she would not take it back. "All sales are final," she said, as she pointed to a tiny sign behind the counter that I hadn't seen the day before. It would have been so easy for her to offer store credit or an even exchange. I would have been happy with that and re-membered next time that all sales items were final. Instead, she lost a customer, I kept the outfit I hated, and told at least seven of my friends about the incident.

Now, every business owner has encountered not just dissatisfied, but truly difficult and demanding customers and clients. What do you do? I have found that taking a detached professional attitude can diffuse a difficult situation and complete the transaction with a minimum of personal upset. In these cases, it is appropriate to be less personable and more efficient. One of the most pow-erful ways to diffuse the situation is to listen fully to the client's complaint and acknowledge how they must be feeling. For example, if the client is upset that your package arrived late, hear him out and then offer a solution. This solution may need to be negotiated a few times. Concentrate on the fix. Listing your reasons why the package arrived late can only escalate the client's upset or simply prolong the resolution process.

39 *"Being in business means working with all types of people, and successful business-people are those who master the art of being appropriate, sincere, and accountable."*

In short, as a small-business owner, you need to make sure that your customers feel served, and that they know they can count on you to deliver. It is much easier, and less costly, to keep a customer than to generate a new one. Being in business means working with all types of people, and successful businesspeople are those who master the art of being appropriate, sincere, and accountable.

Now it's your turn. What is your customer service plan? As I have mentioned before, ask your customers what they think when you are contemplating a change or improvement in service or products. Consider an informal survey that includes only two to three questions. You might include a thank-you-for-your-business note along with a self-addressed stamped envelope, or send an e-mail.

Questions might include:

- Describe what you like about our service or product.

- On a scale from 1 (poor) to 5 (superior), how would you rate our customer service? Comments:

- Is there an additional service or product you would like to see us offer?

- What would you say to recommend us to a friend or colleague?

You could also ask whether they would be willing for you to use their comments as testimonials. Leave a space for them to sign their name for approval.

This gives both satisfied and dissatisfied customers an opportunity to voice compliments and concerns.

Truly the only way to improve and offer exceptional service is your willingness to listen to your customers and make appropriate changes. Customers are loyal when they feel appreciated and feel welcome to voice their thoughts, ideas, and suggestions.

One added benefit of listening to your customers is an increase in referrals. Since word of mouth is essentially free, you may be able to cut your marketing budget, which in turn increases your profit, even if your yearly sales increase only modestly!

Some customers are loyal, yet many are occasional or casual customers. Since investing in your customers can increase your profitability and growth, here are some techniques for turning your customers into sales ambassadors:

- Quality customer service begins with your employees. Train and motivate your staff, especially in effective communication skills. Employees are top priority since each and every employee "touches" your customer in some way. Help make it very positive.

- Pay attention to the details. Doing the daily tasks just 2 percent better makes a huge overall difference.

- Make sure your staff knows your customer-service plan. It's a team effort. If your policy is to respond to customer inquiries within 24 hours, make sure every member of the team is on board.

- Make it easy, pleasant, and fun to do business with you. Create a welcoming atmosphere in person, on the phone, or even via e-mail.

- A smile goes a very long way—even on the phone!

- Invite customers to make referrals and reward them when they do.

- Add to this list with exactly what works for your business.

—— How to Cultivate That "Something —— Special" in Your Business

HAVE YOU EVER WALKED into a store and instantly felt a pleasing warmth and friendliness that made your shopping experience wonderful? Did you notice that something special was going on—but you couldn't quite put your finger on it? I call this "something special feeling" the inner ecology of the business environment.

What Is Inner Ecology?

Just like it is very important to have balance and harmony in nature for a healthy, thriving physical ecology, it is equally important to have balance and harmony in the "inner ecology" or interior landscape of a business owner and the employees. When balance and harmony are present, it breeds teamwork, appreciation, respect, and promotes positive and long-lasting relationships in the workplace and with customers—which is the basis of a successful business. It is this synergy of body, mind, and soul in both the owner and employees that creates positive energy in the business.

This balanced "inner ecology" is often what's missing in a business. When you love your work, you pour your heart into the office environment, and anyone entering feels it. This pouring of heart—just from the sheer joy of sharing—creates the kind of environment that is palpable to customers and they feel it and respond to it.

Inner ecology is actually the relationship between your actions and your understanding of what makes you tick. Ask yourself: How well do I truly know myself? What motivates me? Do I follow my dreams? Do I find peace and joy in what I do? The more you understand what makes you tick, the more present and available you become to life in general. This presence and availability energizes those around you and produces a harmonious work environment. It also stimulates your inner resources of energy, creativity, cooperation, integrity, and confidence.

What Are the Benefits?

Business is built on relationships. Have you noticed that when the boss is open and happy, the employees tend to be happy—and that when the employees are happy, the customers are happy? Happy customers spend money and come back again and again and send their friends.

A smile, a kind word, even a friendly explanation of the store policy would have made a friend and a repeat customer.

As the business owner, it's essential to do good work and treat customers well, but there's more to think about. It's also important to know where you, as the business owner, are coming from. Who are you being in business? How is your inner ecology being expressed? Are you out to get all the business you can with no regard to whose toes you may be stepping on? Do you create extra problems in your attempt to make budget or hit sales targets? Are you able to see the bigger long-term picture for your business?

I have found that most successful businesses are about building relationships—one to one, season after season. When I connect with a client, they connect with me, and the relationship begins. I have found in my business that when my intention is to serve others, I not only help my clients solve problems but I learn and feel served in the process—and clients keep showing up!

In today's economy, businesses sell similar products and services. What distinguishes one business from another today is the quality of the service, and service is expressed through individuals. For example, genuine kindness always sells and is always in fashion.

> **40** "What distinguishes one business from another today is the quality of the service, and service is expressed through individuals."

Inner ecology is a new paradigm—one that is value-based. It comes from your intention of being focused on how you're *being* in your business rather than on what you're *doing* in your business. It puts human connection and service on an equal footing with business results and profits—and the business thrives.

A Real Entrepreneur Story

On her business card, Donis Rothstein of Tobiano, in Jacksonville, Oregon, describes her women's clothing store as an "inviting boutique offering

European styles and gracious assistance." Donis says that the key to her success for the last fifteen years in a small town off the beaten track is twofold:

1. Her reputation for having an artistic eye for style in selecting the clothes for her boutique.

2. Treating customers both new and repeat so they feel welcomed, comfortable, and enjoy a fun experience in her store.

Donis exemplifies inner ecology. How does she accomplish this?

For Donis it comes naturally to be warm, attentive, and friendly. She easily engages customers in creative conversation geared toward an interest they express while they shop and chat. The result is that each customer feels special. Donis makes it easy and fun to shop there. It might be her attention to individual needs, by helping the customer put an outfit together that looks fabulous as well as by being honest about outfits that don't flatter her. Donis's mantra is that the customer is always right. Donis has created an artful ambiance with clothing well displayed, wonderful background music, a comfortable sofa and magazines on a table for friends or especially for husbands. She accepts returns without questions (even sale items), and she sends birthday gifts to her local clients and cards to her customers at a distance. She also periodically calls her local customers to let them know about new clothes that might be of particular interest to them. Donis makes a point of learning her customers' names and greets them by name each time they visit. If she recognizes someone but can't remember their name, she is not embarrassed to ask. Yet the customers always enjoy that she remembers them.

This harmonious style of interacting extends to her staff. Donis always hires staff from referrals and sometimes from local customers. She says, "I honor their abilities and give them a few basic guidelines and let them just do it. I never assume I know more than they do." Also, she gives very specific feedback about what they do well. Donis notes that other merchants in her town have a lot of turnover of sales staff, but she doesn't. She pays her salespeople well and offers additional sales commissions, which motivates them to sell more. To her one full-time employee, Donis offers a yearly bonus, pays for her to go with her on one to two buying trips per year, and offers her clothes at cost. The atmosphere that Donis and her staff create is upbeat, fun, comfortable, friendly, and full of laughter. It helps people to feel truly valued and served.

How Can You Cultivate Inner Ecology?

Instead of using attack-defense strategies that raise your blood pressure and increase your lawyer's fees while you're trying to increase your bottom line, try the following to cultivate and nurture the inner ecology within you:

1. Accept the challenge and move forward by being open to a variety of possibilities. Choose one and try it. If it doesn't work, try the next possibility. Be like water that effortlessly changes course to move around obstacles. Stay open.

2. Cultivate your own natural wisdom to solve problems. Have faith in yourself and your team's good ideas. Set a plan and implement it, trusting that you and your team will be able to handle any and all results.

    41 "Have faith in your own ideas and abilities. If you don't believe in yourself it's hard for others to believe in you."

3. Let go of past resentments, beliefs, values, judgments, and opinions about products, clients, and yourself that are no longer useful in promoting your business with confidence. This often is the hardest to do consistently because we are trained to look at the past to predict the future. Handle what is happening now, and know that the right next step will become clear. Be sure to take it.

4. Approach all business dealings with the attitude of the glass being half full rather than half empty. For example, always greet clients with a smile rather than a frown.

5. Spend more time asking questions and listening to your clients with the intention of building a relationship, not just selling your service or products. Be present and available to listen to the customers with spaciousness and respect. You will stand out among your competitors by actually delivering what your clients asked for while exceeding their expectations in some special way.

By getting to know yourself a little better and trying some of these ideas, you will start to make the shift to seeing the amazing possibilities within your own inner ecology. You will have greater access to the wealth of natural wisdom that is within you and guides you on your journey.

How to Warm Up to Cold Calls

MARKETING AND SALES are the lifeblood of any business. Marketing means everything you do to secure your position within your market segment. Your market includes the total possibilities for generating revenues for your products and services.

What, then, is sales? Simply put, sales is *bringing in the business*—the revenue that produces the profit for your company. Every business owner has their own style of making sales. However, at some point as a business owner, you will face making cold calls.

When I ask my clients what scares them the most about starting their own business, many say "selling myself," or "I hate making cold calls." Even people who are already in business often say that they like talking to their friends, current clients, and colleagues about their business and enjoy working on their projects once they make a deal, but they dread making cold calls.

Here are some practical tips gleaned from my experience and those of my clients and colleagues for making cold calls work for you:

1. *Make each cold call a warm call.* The easiest way is to use a contact name and say, "Mary Smith suggested I call you." If you don't have a referral, write a letter with a special offer. Follow up your letter with a call and make reference to your letter. Always do your research on the contact company. Use information gleaned from your research to establish a connection when you call. Talk about an issue facing their company, and focus on their needs.

2. *Choose a time of day when you are most energetic to make your calls.* Plan the number of calls for that day, take a deep breath, sit up straight, and do them all at once. This creates a momentum. One suggestion made to a colleague of mine makes sense: Make five calls each day. You feel nervous before the first call, you feel better after the second call, you feel confident after the third call, you feel great after the fourth call, and you feel successful after the fifth call. This is regardless of the outcome of each call, because you reached your goal of five calls a day. The calls will get easier each day, and you will get results.

3. *Write a script for your calls.* You may want to write one script for voicemail and another script for talking live. There is a difference between the two, and you want to be prepared for both. The purpose

of a script is to clarify what you want to say. Practice your script so that you can remember the points you want to make. You will change what you say to each person you talk to, but you will remember what you want to say and do it naturally.

4. *Stay organized with a contact-management system.* You can keep track of each contact and the result, as well as make notes about pertinent information and when and how to follow up. If you tell someone you will call them back on a certain day, make sure that you call them back on that day, and with the information you promised. A system will help you remember.

5. *Be a problem solver.* People are looking for solutions to their problems. Don't push for a close on your first call. Ask for a meeting to explore their needs and how your service or business can provide them with solutions. Sell benefits, not features.

6. *Think about how you like to be "sold."* Develop your presentation around that. Be natural and conversational, and ask questions so that you can tailor what you have to offer to fit the customer's needs.

7. *Don't forget to smile.* Studies have shown that a smile travels across phone lines and creates a positive impression.

Discover a sales style that suits you. A key to sales success is to choose your strategy and put it into action consistently.

42 *"A key to sales success is to choose your strategy and put it into action consistently."*

Landing Consulting Gigs

LIFE AS A CONSULTANT or independent contractor often involves interviewing frequently for consulting projects with a variety of companies. One mistake consultants make is sticking with one large contract with one company; then, when that contract ends, they have no clients, no network, and not many prospects. This is why it is essential to market yourself even when you are busy with current projects and clients. Remember, you are selling your expertise and ability to solve your client's problems.

How to Stand Out and Win the Contract

Be prepared to answer these questions clearly, concisely, and powerfully:

- What can you offer us? What are your value-added skills, industry knowledge, and successes?

- How are your services unique? Why should we contract with your company?

- Given our expectations and our company culture, please explain how you plan to interact with our team so that you can solve our problem productively and efficiently?

- Who recommended you?

- Can we talk to some of your past clients?

Faith in your own ideas and abilities, and your willingness to take an independent position in the face of opposition or possible conflict are essential qualities. If you don't believe in yourself it's hard for others to believe in you.

For example, I recently was asked to give a recommendation for a colleague for a contract position. When I asked why they were so interested in my colleague, they said that they felt that she was confident and very competent even though she hadn't worked with an organization exactly like theirs before.

After you have landed the contract make sure you display these often highly valued competencies:

- *Taking Responsibility for Your Performance.* Set realistic goals and implement, get feedback, and deal with issues promptly.

- *Technological Savvy.* It is essential to keep up with what's new in the industry so you can assist clients in learning new complicated programs.

- *Analytical Problem Solving.* Tackle a problem by using a logical, systematic, sequential approach. Anticipate and be prepared for possible contingencies.

- *Fostering Teamwork.* Demonstrate interest, skill, and success in getting groups to work productively together.

- *Flexibility.* Be open to different and new ways of doing things. Be willing to modify your preferred way of doing things by thinking out of the box and seeing the merits of others' perspectives.

• *Managing Change.* Be able to see the big picture and how what you do fits within the company. Demonstrate support for innovation and organizational changes to improve effectiveness; initiate, sponsor, and implement as well as help others successfully manage organizational change. Realize that there is often a continued need for rapid change.

• *Communication and Interpersonal Skills.* Keep multiple channels of communication open within the organization; present and write well. Be able to influence others to gain support for ideas and solutions. Be sensitive and aware of interests and important concerns of others you are working with. Develop a working understanding of cultural differences and needs, essential given today's global nature of business.

Being prepared and confident are the keys to landing a consulting contract. Here are some tips to help you:

Tips

• Ask yourself: Which key competencies do I have? Leverage those to sell yourself. Build on your strengths. Highlight successes in previous consulting projects. Have six to eight success stories to use when making your presentation to a potential client. Past performance is considered the best predictor of future performance.

• Do research on the company and the players before you meet with them. Know their challenges. Think of ways you can offer solutions to their specific problems or issues.

• Show what you can do for the company. What benefits do you bring? How will you boost the bottom line? Offer other benefits, such as saving money, saving time, making life easier for managers, improving relationships, and increasing customer satisfaction.

• Be professional when leaving your first voicemail message, it may be your first impression. (Don't do this: I once got a message from a consultant, who said: "Someone told me you had a need for a business consultant. I don't know what it is but please call me back.")

• Display confidence and composure. Script, practice, and believe in yourself. It's contagious.

• Ask for the contract. Ask for next steps before you leave. Make sure you have answered or asked for any concerns the decision maker may have. Don't leave the meeting with someone having a question about you.

- Be authentic. Define your service clearly. Explain the benefits of working with you—why you are unique. Follow up after presentations and express your interest.

- When you get the written contract, make sure that the scope of work and payment schedule are detailed. Also, outline in writing the plan for dealing with additions and extra work hours on the contract. Have all parties sign and date the contract agreement.

How Do You Stand Out?

Finally, before you put any marketing materials or presentations together, do this exercise to gain clarity on what makes you stand out as a consultant. Think carefully about the following questions:

1. Describe exactly what you offer. What is your unique expertise?

2. What success stories really show how you work with clients/customers?

3. What solutions could you offer your ideal clients/customers that your competitors can't offer? What other solutions do you offer?

4. What do your customers/clients say about you?

Now incorporate the answers to these questions into your core marketing message in your presentations.

Dealing with Downtime in Your Business

FOR MANY BUSINESSES, the busiest time of the year is the holiday season. Yet for some entrepreneurs, that's the slowest time of the year. All businesses experience seasonal income ups and downs, but for entrepreneurs it's usually feast or famine from late November until the end of December. In which category does your business fall? If your business is feasting, get your running shoes ready and prepare for the marathon. If your business is hungry, it may be time for creative belt-tightening. Here are ten tips for taking control of your downtime while creating business for the New Year.

10 Tips for Taking Control of Your Downtime

1. Take stock of your products and services. Be very specific as to what worked and what did not. Decide what to keep, improve, or delete. If you are a one-person business, this can be a difficult process. Think about hiring a consultant to assist you. You need to take an honest look at which of your services are in demand and which need some zip. As only one person, you must spend time on those services that have a high payoff. You may need to give up a pet project for which there isn't a viable market.

2. Get organized. For example, budget time to update your customer mailing list. Learn a new database or contact-management system that will improve access and maintenance, so that you can communicate quickly and easily with your customers.

3. Attend a professional organization's holiday events. If you only want to go to one such event, pick the group whose function you've been meaning to attend but haven't as yet. You'll make new contacts and possibly gain new perspectives and ideas for your business.

4. Reconnect with your professional and personal networks. Update them on your business progress and new services. Explore how you might do some strategic partnering. After all, out of sight is out of mind. Your contacts won't refer business to you if they haven't heard from you in a year. *Reminder*: It's best to do this regularly throughout the year. Set aside time each week for networking. Write it in your calendar now.

5. Write a newsletter. Plan to mail or e-mail it after January 5th, so that your newsletter is one of the first pieces of mail your clients see when they return to work after the holidays. Plan to produce a monthly or quarterly newsletter. If this is too daunting, team up with an owner of a complementary business and produce a joint newsletter. Pick a theme for each newsletter and contribute information from your unique perspectives. Business owners I know who write regular newsletters say that they gain new perspectives and ideas for their businesses and that their volume of business increases significantly after each newsletter.

6. Request testimonials from current and past customers. Besides making you feel better when business is slow, you will have testimonials on hand to share with prospective customers to include in a new brochure, a newsletter, a proposal, and conference materials. An easy way to get your request returned is to include a form with one or two questions for your customers, asking what they liked about your service. Be sure

also to include a question about what they would like to see improved. Include a line for them to sign to grant you permission to use their testimonial in your materials. Don't forget to include a self-addressed stamped envelope.

7. Offer to do project work for other business owners in your personal network who may be swamped during the holiday season. Or bid several projects with a deadline in November. This will bring in cash during your slow season.

8. Review your business and marketing plans. Revise as needed. Write your goals for next year. Then write the steps you need to take to reach those goals. Put benchmark dates in your calendar to check up on yourself. Do a specific, prioritized, action-item list for January.

9. Put balance in your life. Spend more time with your family and friends. Do those leisure activities for which you didn't have time during the year. Relax, and give yourself permission to enjoy your time off. Similarly, if you do get unexpected time off throughout the year, take advantage of it.

> **43** "Put balance in your life. Spend more time with your family and friends. Do those leisure activities for which you didn't have time during the year."

10. Plan ahead for the slow season next year. Project how you can meet your financial goals during the rest of the year. Take a well-earned vacation in December.

CHAPTER 6

GET CONNECTED TO THE WEB FOR PROFIT

Keep-in-Touch Marketing Using the Internet

WHAT IS KEEP-IN-TOUCH MARKETING? Simply it is each time you contact a customer. Because 80 percent of business comes from 20 percent of your customers, keep in touch with that 20 percent as often as possible. These are interested customers that are looking for or inclined to purchase your service or particular product because they already know you and trust you.

44 *"Because 80 percent of business comes from 20 percent of your customers, keep in touch with that 20 percent as often as possible."*

However, each "touch" needs to respect the customer by including more than a sales pitch. In fact, there may not be a sales pitch at all. For example, it may be suggestions and tips on how to make life easy for your customers. However, all communication includes your business name and contact information. This type of marketing works equally well for Internet businesses as well as for "brick-and-mortar" businesses that also have a Web presence. Some of the ways to keep in touch and in front of your targeted customers are offering free newsletters, special reports, or monthly inspirational quotes that provide relevant information and serve as a platform to promote and sell e-courses, e-books, and other products and services.

The free offerings and resources develop a relationship with your customers. Because they need to get comfortable with you, people rarely buy on the first visit to your site. In order to stay in touch and keep your name in front of them, you want your site visitors to opt in to your e-mail list.

What is an opt-in e-mail list? On the Web, this means that your customers agree to be on your list and to receive information or subscribe to your e-newsletter via e-mail. There are two desired outcomes of keep-in-touch marketing with an opt-in list:

1. Build a large quality e-mail list of customers who like your informative offerings.

2. Sell products and services and offer free resources.

David Riklan of SelfGrowth.com, a master at keep-in-touch marketing, has 950,000 (and counting) subscribers on his opt-in e-mail list. He offers weekly e-newsletters on self-improvement and natural health. David says, "To be successful on the Internet, my mantra is, 'Build your list and take massive action!'"

How do you build a quality e-mail list that has the quantity to bring dollars into your business and the quality to keep subscribers?

According to David Riklan, the conversion rate of a visitor to a subscriber is approximately 4 percent. In other words, you need 100 visitors to get 4 subscribers. Your goal is to convert as many visitors to your website as possible to become subscribers to your e-newsletter and ultimately to create a strong list of buyers. An e-newsletter sent weekly, monthly, or quarterly is most frequently used to build an opt-in e-mail list. Create visible and inviting ways for your site visitors to subscribe to your e-newsletter such as:

1. *Use incentives.* For example, a visitor receives a free CD, an e-book, or a special report as a gift for signing up for the free e-newsletter. To put them at ease, make sure that you have a privacy policy and assure your visitors that you will not sell their names.

2. *Buy lists that fit your target market.* This can be expensive (i.e., $0.05 to $1 per subscriber or $0.10 or more per name for a one-time mailing).

3. *Add "Tell a friend" to your e-newsletter or e-special report.* Provide good content and your subscribers will tell others by forwarding your e-newletter or report.

4. *Optimize your website for search engine placement.* This is called search engine optimization (SEO). You can do this yourself or hire a company to do it for you. Research this carefully and decide what makes the most sense in time, money, and results. There are two basic ways to improve search engine listings:

- *Use keywords or meta tags on each page to attract search robots.* Meta tags (keywords) are HTML placeholders inside your code that can be found at the top of each page of your website. To help the search engines, you may want to target three to five key meta phrases per page, but no more. Make sure that the keywords you choose for each page also appear at least two times near the top of the page. Use a few keywords that are intuitive for someone searching for your type of business, such as, "Career coach in San Francisco Bay Area." Make sure the title of your website contains the primary keyword for which you want search engines to rank the page. Resubmit your website to major search engines about every four to six weeks.

- *Use reciprocal links.* Contact webmasters of similar sites in your industry that are not direct competitors and offer them a link in return for providing you with one. Search engines use the popularity of your site as a relevant criterion. In other words, it is important how many quality websites link to and from your page. One way to quickly get quality links, which count more for optimization than quantity, is by getting listed in Web directories, such as those offered by your local Chamber of Commerce or Better Business Bureau chapter, or professional directories that charge an annual fee for the service.

Although getting listed high on search engines is important, you do not want to spend all your efforts in doing just that. *Remember:* Ask for help from those that have more expertise than you do to accomplish your search engine optimization plan.

Technical savvy is crucial but it is only one side of the marketing story—it is how you implement your strategy. The other side of the story is having a well-thought-out brand and marketing plan. But even this is not the whole story. You need to be crystal clear as to what you want your customers to experience, how you are differentiated from your competitors, and that what you offer your customers is of value and not only builds your customer list but, more importantly, builds your business. Yet all this is still not enough. You need to take action and do it consistently.

Tips from Tech-Savvy Entrepreneurs

THERE ARE MANY WAYS to use technology in small businesses: promotion and marketing; shopping carts to sell products; reservations for lodging, restaurants, and travel; software programs designed specifically for a particular type of business (i.e., point-of-sale programs for restaurants and retail stores); or systematizing and streamlining office processes to add value in services to customers.

Because I always learn more when I talk with people in the small-business trenches about their experiences and successes, I have gleaned some tips on how to successfully use technology to build your business and provide superior service as well as streamline business processes:

Tip 1

Combine a user-friendly website with caring customer service. The majority of small businesses today have a website. When you are building or redesigning your website, here are some key questions to consider:

45 *"Combine a user-friendly website with caring customer service."*

- How well is it working for your business now?

- Are prospective clients discovering you through the Web because your company is listed on the first page of a Google search?

- Is it compelling enough to keep them on your site and purchase or request more information?

- Do you want to sell products or services via your website as a main part of your business model, or is it mainly informational and interactive for your current customers?

- What do your customers want?

It's essential to know very specifically what you want your website to do. Then strategize and build it or add to it to make it happen. Of course, this is easier said than done.

Here are two examples of successful business owners who redesigned the company's website to meet their goals and satisfy their existent and prospective customers.

Anthony Sandberg and Rich Jepson of OCSC Sailing School in Berkeley, California, say that over the years, most of their business has come through word of mouth. When they decided to revise it significantly to include Web-enabled reservations a few years ago, they wanted the website to augment word of mouth. So now, when new customers call the school, they get that warm personal responsive attention that is a trademark of OCSC, but now they can also check the school out via the website. In 2006, OCSC received an award for the best sailing website in the industry. Currently, they plan to update their site every two years and add to it constantly to keep it interesting and very user friendly.

Anthony says, "I think its success has been how we have combined the website with our caring customer service. When we ask new customers how they heard about us, many report like this:

> I heard about you through a friend. I looked you up on the Web and your site was the best I've seen. I called and the front desk people were very helpful and responsive. So, I signed up. The next day I got an e-mail welcoming me to the program. Then a few days later, I got a call confirming my class.

In addition, OCSC has two wireless networks. One is internal to facilitate communication with staff within the company, and the other one is external for members and reservations.

Barbara Llewellyn, owner of Barbara Llewellyn Catering and Special Events in Oakland, California, believes that pictures sell. Generally people surfing the Web for caterers don't have time for reading a lot of words. Therefore, her company's website is full of beautiful photos with one-line descriptions that speak volumes about their food, service, presentation, and quality. Her website is an online brochure. Barbara shares that "Many of my customers look forward to the recipes that we update regularly. Also, we include a Radio/TV and Media link of our appearances and talks. This definitely adds credibility and makes it easy for media folks to find us."

Tip 2

If you are technically oriented and inventive, you might develop a technical gadget that solves customers' problems quickly and saves them time and money, which leads to great word of mouth for your business. Michael Dennison of Bavarian Professionals in Berkeley, California, is a good example of this:

Michael specializes in repairing BMWs. Cars have very technical systems now and there are many, many possible problems that can occur, which can be different for every make and model. If the mechanics have seen the same technical problem five times before, they can fix a car faster and more efficiently. In addition, there are intermittent problems that are hard to diagnose. For this purpose Michael developed and built a device he calls a "Glitch Catcher." It's like an airplane's black box in that it acts as a data logger. For the hard-to-diagnose problems, Michael puts the "Glitch Catcher" in a customer's car, All the customer needs to do is push the button when, for example, she hears the sound. It captures the data, which is then put on an Excel spreadsheet. The problem is diagnosed and fixed. As Michael explains, "This is extremely helpful because the next time a car comes in with a weird problem, we've seen it before and we can fix it with an hour of labor instead of repeat visits over weeks or months! This is one of the reasons that most of our business is word of mouth."

Tip 3

Do what it takes to learn how to use 95 percent of the capability of your expensive software applications. Make sure they interface with each other for efficiency and ease of communication within your business.

Most business owners use only 5 percent of the capability of their systems. But don't be discouraged. Remember my earlier advice about not being a lone wolf? If you are not technically savvy or don't want to learn how to become proficient on your systems, hire a company that has the expertise to set up your systems for you and train you and your staff how to use them effectively and efficiently.

For example, one client of mine, Alasdair Clements, says his company, GoCar Tours, is "big into technology." Since they have two locations in San Francisco, franchise locations in Miami and San Diego, and are planning to expand internationally, Alasdair has automated systems that allow staff and franchisees to connect remotely. That way they can get all the information they need in order to automate the same systems as the home office, as well as easily access training on how to run the franchise business and communicate more efficiently.

Tip 4

You don't need to have all of your applications in-house, you can contract with cutting-edge Web companies whose database, marketing, and sales systems will give you leverage in getting ahead of your competition.

For example, many service business entrepreneurs also have products for sale on their website. It is more cost-effective and easier to pay a monthly fee to a vendor to manage your database and shopping cart. Personally, I use one vendor for my monthly e-newsletter, *EZ Steps*, and another vendor for credit card payments and fulfillment. There are many Web service companies that can handle your database, e-newsletter, shopping cart, and credit card payments. Shop around for the company or companies that best fit the needs of your business. Also, ask industry colleagues for recommendations.

Mark Estes of Mark Estes Photography in Oakland, California, is a great example of how to outsource technical expertise to create satisfied customers:

As a photographer Mark Estes knows his business is all about connecting with people and creating distinctive images. These images need to be easily accessible to his clients for viewing and purchasing. His motto is "A picture is worth 1000 words." Mark's website is designed by a Web design company that specializes in building websites for artists and photographers. In this way, Mark is able to focus on what he does best—photographing, marketing, and interacting with customers. The website also presents high-quality portfolios for prospective clients, which can be updated and changed easily. Mark connects with his clients person to person and then refers them to his website to show his work style and range. One key technical feature is the ability to easily and quickly change images daily, especially on the home page, which enables Mark to promote any area of his business.

How has this helped Mark's business? Since the website is built to load photo files very quickly (under 3 seconds), it is easy to put current projects on his website to show the variety of his work to prospective customers. Speedy response to a customer's request helps Mark stand out in his field.

Instead of or along with a business card, Mark gives photo books to prospective clients or colleagues who might have the opportunity to refer him. He uses an online publishing company (there are many) and easily creates an inexpensive photo book of up to twenty pages. Mark says, "I like to make a $2\frac{1}{2}$ by $3\frac{1}{2}$" soft-cover book. I put one photo per page with text, and then add my logo and contact information on the front and/or back cover. It's a great promotional tool and only costs me $1 per book. It's very easy and quick to make, which makes it so much more fun to give out than a business card and asking someone to log onto a website."

If you have been in business more than two years and you find that you are spending more time on the technical aspects of your business than on billable hours or project/product sales and service, it's time to seriously consider how you can outsource your business's technical needs. Try some of the tips in this chapter!

Six Ways to Promote Your Business via the Web

THE INTERNET IS a great cost-effective way to promote your business. However, it seems daunting because:

- There are not millions but billions of websites jockeying for position and attention.

- Trillions of pieces of e-mail are sent out each year.

- The average person is bombarded with thousands of advertising messages every day from TV, radio, the Internet, and billboards.

Two things your website must have for your business to stand out in the overcrowded Internet space:

1. Compelling website copy with solid content and attention-grabbing headlines that your target market is searching for on the Web. Make sure your website doesn't appear to be only about selling something. People want information, not hype.

   46 *"Make sure your website doesn't appear to be only about selling something. People want information, not hype."*

2. A way to capture site visitors' contact information. Your site must get net-surfers to stay long enough to view an "opt-in" offer that is irresistible—like a special report or teleseminar—so that they will join your mailing list. You can then start a relationship with your prospects. Most of your online marketing and sales will come from this e-mail list.

Jadon Wellman, manager of Web Marketing for Small Businesses at Hewlett Packard, says:

The key to Web marketing is to respect the customer's agenda. The focus is always on the customer. People think if you build it they will come. Not so.

Find out what your customers want, find out where they are on the Web and then go "talk" with them on blogs or forums or your own website and let them know about you. Start building a relationship, and let customers know clearly and briefly how your service or product might solve their problem(s). It's also important to be humble when you design your website. You think you know what your customers want. You don't. Ask them. Do informal usability tests, get feedback, and build it into your site.

I recommend that if you are not a writer, and especially if you have no clue about how to write compelling Web copy, that you hire a Web consultant or writer who can help you. Remember, you're in the business of providing your expert advice, product, or service, and your website needs to work for you. Don't pinch pennies here or be a lone wolf. Your job is to develop the promotional strategy that works best for your company and target market.

Consider using a combination of these strategies:

1. *Create online press releases that drive traffic if not lots of free publicity.* Most small-business owners believe that their press releases won't be noticed or picked up by big media outlets. They are most likely correct, but that doesn't mean that a well-written press release with an engaging story line could not create significant increases in site traffic and generate hundreds or thousands of incoming links. Remember, incoming links improve your website's popularity, which search engines use to move your site up in Internet searches. There are online wire services that are fee-based (businesswire.com) or free (prweb.com) for distribution of your press releases. This is much less expensive than a pay-per-click ad campaign. As an added bonus, you could get free publicity from the media. It is worth considering in your promotional campaign because you gain credibility as an expert in your field as well as visibility. *Remember:* Press releases that are thinly disguised ads will land in the trash.

2. *Submit articles to websites that cater to your target market.* Do you want to become known as an expert in your field? Think about publishing well-researched, content-rich, helpful articles in others' e-zines or newsletters, or in other websites relevant to your industry and/or your target market. This gives you wider presence on the Web and builds your reputation. After all, your articles do not ONLY appear on your own website.

   Research Web e-newsletters carefully to determine their quality and how well they match your market. This takes more time, but it pays off in the end. Try to avoid the scattergun approach of submitting to websites that have a large quantity of e-zines and newsletters that are on a wide variety of topics, many of which will be unrelated to what your business offers. Consider creating a joint venture with another Internet website that is in a similar market niche but not a direct competitor. You can promote your e-newsletter, e-book, or special report on their site and they can promote theirs on your site. This works best also with people who have a similar-size e-mail list to yours. If you have 100 people on your list and you ask a list owner who has 100,000 people on their list, they most likely won't be motivated to joint venture with you.

3. *Create a blog that keeps your business "top of mind" with customers.* A blog is a powerful, cost-effective alternative to a website or e-mail newsletter. Your information can be fresh, up-to-date, targeted, and sent easily to your niche market(s). You can also create more than one blog, each targeted to a different market. It is a quick and easy way to build your presence on the Web, connect and engage with your current customers, and find new ones. There are online companies that help you set up your blog and make it easy for you to maintain it. Fees for hosting range from $4.95 to $29.95 per month depending on the package you choose. You can also create one for free and maintain it on your own website. Before you start blogging, investigate what you plan to do with your blog, what your focus is, and whom you plan to reach. Research by reading other blogs to get the flavor and spirit of what small-business folks are writing about and asking about.

Blogs are also a great way to "listen" to your customers, because you can pose questions and ask for feedback. A blog is also your platform, a way to express what you stand for, publicize your expertise, and present your ideas while building a relationship and trust with your readers. Your blog needs to be congruent with your marketing plan; make it part of the cohesive business you've built around a single market serving their needs. Be careful with self-promotion. You can list products and services at the bottom of the blog and occasionally mention specific products. In the latter case, include a "click here icon to learn more," which can lead to a sales page. One added benefit of a well-positioned, interesting, and informative blog is that many major media folks look for stories and experts by reading blogs.

If you're not ready to create your own blog and update it regularly (two to four times per week), try this: Research and identify those quality blogs that relate to your industry and target market; to find out which blogs have a lot of traffic go to www.alexa.com. Then identify three to five quality blogs and post solutions to problems raised or sim-

ply enter the discussion. Always include your name, business, and website in your signature. If you have a blog, invite readers to go to your
blog for more information. This way, you are becoming visible on the
Web and are building credibility without maintaining your own blog.
For small or solo business owners, it may be overwhelming to maintain
a quality, engaging, and information-rich blog.

4. *Make strategic use of pay-per-click advertising.* What is pay-per-click
advertising? Pay-per-click (PPC) is an Internet advertising model in
which advertisers only pay when a user actually clicks on an ad to visit
the advertiser's website. Advertisers bid on keywords that they think
their particular target market would use to search for a product or service. When someone types a keyword query matching the advertiser's
keyword list, the advertiser's ad may appear on the search results page.
These ads are known as sponsored ads and appear next to—and sometimes above—search engine organic results on the page. The advertiser
pays only when the user clicks on the ad.

As an advertiser you can expect to pay from $0.01 up to $0.50 or
more per click. Very popular search terms can cost much more on popular engines. The purpose is to drive traffic to your website so that
your ad will be seen by billions. It is critical that your ad clearly states
what problems you solve and lists the key benefits for buyers. Users
are specifically searching for a particular service or product. If your
PPC campaign is well targeted, you will reach an engaged and ready
audience.

The small-business challenge is that keyword search is everyone's
front door into the Internet. And it's hard to compete against the big companies who can pay more for keywords. Therefore, it is essential that you
choose a unique phrase that applies specifically to your business. For example: Somatic massage therapist in Phoenix.Try out several phrases; just
like a market niche, they can't be too broad or too narrow.

As you can see, it is extremely important to research how PPC
will benefit your business, and especially how it fits into your marketing budget. Be sure to carefully track the ROI (return on investment).
It is very likely that you could be paying more in advertising than you
receive in sales. Start small and set a deadline for evaluating how well
it is working. Track results carefully and decide whether it works. If
not, stop the ads!

5. *Advertise in e-zines or e-newsletters for high and frequent exposure.*
When you place an advertisement in a high-profile e-newsletter targeted

to your same market, it is more likely that it will be read because the reader has requested the newsletter and trusts the source. It is also cost-effective. Research newsletters carefully and choose wisely. Then track the results of your ads. Keep running the ads that work and cancel those that don't work as well for you. In many e-newsletters the ads appear near the top of the page before the featured articles. *Remember*: It is a waste of money to run an ad only one time. Repeat exposure is what works best in advertising.

6. *Practice social or online networking.* What is it? According to *Webster's Dictionary*, social networking is the use of a website to connect with people who share personal or professional interests, a common place of origin, an education at a particular school, etc. Myspace.com is a well-known site that has become very popular. However, many small-business owners might think that these sites are just for fun. Not so. Social networking sites are becoming more and more popular with business folks who have little time to go to in-person networking events but want to develop a strong network of professional colleagues and make business contacts. Two business-oriented social network sites are Ryze.com and Linkedin.com, for which membership is free. As a member you can post your profile, biography, photos, list your interests, and identify your industry.

The social network sites offer free resources and are very user friendly. You can join groups in your industry or your geographic area. Ryze.com also offers a monthly fee ($9.95) for gold membership, which gives users advanced search capabilities and allows them to set up groups focused on their areas of interest. This is an easy, inexpensive way to make connections and create visibility and credibility. If you have a tight promotion budget, this is a strategy to include.

Which of these strategies fit into your marketing plan and budget? Select one or two to start, go slowly, track results, and stick with the one to two strategies that really work well. *Remember*: It is not about you, it's about your client:

What information do they need?

How do they want to be treated?

What problems can you solve?

What is the benefit to them of working with you?

Once you convert users to buyers, make it easy, fun, and productive for them to work with you, and you'll attract all the clients you want.

——— Your Web Promotion Action Plan ———

AS AN EXERCISE, write two priority goals to accomplish in the next three months for implementing one of your Web promotion objectives.

As we discussed in Chapter 3, the section on Magic Formula, remember to put MAGIC in your goals. This is what MAGIC stands for:

M = **M**easurable

A = **A**ct on to-do list daily

G = **G**oals give your dream a deadline

I = **I**nspire others to assist you

C = **C**onfidence and belief in your self and your abilities

---

WEB PROMOTION ACTION PLAN

Promotion Objective: _____

Goal 1: _____ Due Date: _____

Goal 2: _____ Due Date: _____

Strategies (Examples):

- Technology: Use technology to _____, _____, and _____

- Revenue Model: Generate revenues by _____, _____, and _____

- Markets/Customers: Focus on _____, _____, and _____ markets

- Positioning: Become nationally known for _____

Obstacles: List one to three obstacles that might get in your way:

1. _____

2. _____

3. _____

Daily Habits:

Daily habits are small constructive actions done on a daily routine basis, which can quickly give you a sense of accomplishment and forward momentum. These daily habits form the foundation upon which major change takes place. Examples are exercising, meditating, processing all incoming e-mail daily, following up a call within 24 hours, taking a power nap, writing affirmations, or doing a fun activity with a family member. These constructive habits can be professional or personal.

47 *"Daily habits are small constructive actions done on a daily routine basis, which can quickly give you a sense of accomplishment and forward momentum."*

It has been said that whatever you do daily for 21 days becomes a habit. Why not develop a few constructive habits that will continually propel you forward toward the goal(s) you want to achieve? List several daily habits that would support, energize, and motivate you:

1. _____

2. _____

3. _____

To-Do List for Week of _____ :

1. _____

2. _____

3. _____

Success Stories of Seasoned Web-Based Entrepreneurs

THE INTERNET IS UBIQUITOUS. Yet in 1994, most people didn't know what the Internet was. As Heidi Paul, an Internet pioneer, says, "I had to spell the word 'Internet' to potential clients when trying to make appointments because they had never heard of it or the World Wide Web." Now, almost every entrepreneur and company has a presence on the Web. Instead of printing business cards first, new business owners get a domain name and build a website.

When I started my business in 1995, I printed my business cards, put an ad in the local Yellow Pages, and began attending a multitude of networking events. I didn't know what a domain name was and certainly didn't think I needed a website. Two years later, I had a domain name and a website and jumped into the new world of the Internet. As Mary Foley, founder of The Bodacious Women's Club, says, "What excites me is that the Internet is such a powerful medium that gives everyday entrepreneurs delivery, distribution, and communication systems at price points that they just didn't have before. In short, the Net enables small players to play big." Yes, the Internet levels the playing field of business so that it is much more about ideas and who can deliver the best services to specific niches.

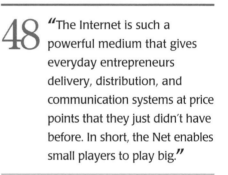

48 *"The Internet is such a powerful medium that gives everyday entrepreneurs delivery, distribution, and communication systems at price points that they just didn't have before. In short, the Net enables small players to play big."*

The three Web-based entrepreneurs I profile in this chapter may have brick-and-mortar offices, but their shingle is their website and most of their business is conducted via the Internet. Each one illustrates a different business model that successfully generates revenue and profits. Most importantly, as I have discovered with most entrepreneurs, they are more than willing to share their wisdom, experience, and hard-won advice.

Heidi Paul

Heidi Paul is cofounder with Frank Forbes of WineCountry.com, a wine country destination Web portal featuring Napa Valley and Sonoma in California.

Heidi definitely considers herself to be an accidental entrepreneur. After resigning from a small high-tech firm to take the summer off and then find a new corporate job, she agreed to help Frank, her significant other, with marketing and sales for a few months to get him started. As she says, "For the first 10 years I still thought I would go back to the corporate world. One day it dawned on me, that I'm an entrepreneur and I actually like it, and I've done whatever it takes to build a successful Internet business!"

Their business model is based on advertising by accommodation venues, wineries, restaurants, and other tourist destinations. WineCountry.com has two sets of customers:

1. Advertisers who generate their revenue

2. Users or consumers who get information from the site

Over the years, emphasis has been on building up traffic on their site; currently 3 million people visit the site per year. Their advertisers know the value that this amount of traffic and brand name provides them. Online advertising is validated by tracking how many hits leave WineCountry's site and click on the advertisers' sites. Heidi says, "The advertisers understand that it is our job to get the consumers to their sites and it is their job to convert them into buyers. For our consumers, we are always connecting them with and adding to our offerings so that they think of us as the premier destination Web portal for Napa and Sonoma wine country."

Crossroads in Business.   As any company grows, big challenges occur that might mean radically changing the products and services offered, or closing the business. Also, it is always a challenge to know how many employees to hire and who are the "right people" with the exact skill sets most important for the company to meet their goals. One common problem of all entrepreneurial businesses is depending too heavily on one large client. This was the case for Heidi. WineCountry lost their biggest client. At the time, they offered Web design, hosting, and marketing, and their biggest client company generated $300,000 per year. They had 25 employees. It is always a very difficult decision to lay off employees even when it is absolutely necessary for the business to survive. Heidi explains, "It is heart wrenching to make a decision that affects people's lives. After the layoff, I met with those employees who remained to answer questions and grieve, and also to let them know the new direction of the company."

In business, the key is the willingness to make changes, big or small. Many business owners might choose to throw in the towel when faced with a big loss in their business. That's when what motivates you in business and being passionate about your business propels you to continue, even when facing huge challenges. As Heidi says, "I am driven to succeed and I am completely unwilling to fail. I thrive on solving business problems creatively for ourselves and our clients."

Taking calculated risks is also one of the traits of successful entrepreneurs. Heidi and her partner, Frank, decided to phase out Web design, hosting, and marketing online for client companies, and to shift to building up their advertising revenue. Now WineCountry is 90 percent marketing and 10 percent Web design. Instead of client companies bringing in revenue of between $50,000 and $300,000 per year, they need many more customers because their average advertising customer brings in $200 a month.

Heidi proudly shares, "It worked and now our revenue is much higher. The shift in our business offerings paid off. I know it's surprising but we did not take funding during the crazy dot-com days and we managed to survive the bust. To this day we continually refine our business and develop strategies to roll with the many changes in the Internet world to survive and thrive!"

Hard-Won Advice for Other Business Owners

- Understand what you're willing to risk and sacrifice doing it—personal wealth, hours of sleep, time with family and friends, vacations.

- Be willing to have a mentor or two and offer a great product.

- It often takes longer and costs are much higher than you projected.

- In a fast-growing start-up, it is as important to react to opportunities as it is to focus on business goals. Constant reaction can take you away from your mission and focus.

Mary Foley and Cheryl Thompson

Mary Foley and Cheryl Thompson are cohosts of the BodaciousWomensClub .com, an online club for businesswomen who want to be outrageously in charge of their lives. The club provides an easy and fun way to connect with other bodacious women for inspiration, courage, and laughter.

One of the beauties of an Internet-based business is that it can be located anywhere and that partners can live in different locations. Mary is based in Richmond, Virginia, and Cheryl is based in Lee's Summit, Missouri.

Mary didn't actually set out to start an Internet business. After leaving a ten-year career at AOL, she decided to share her major lesson learned—"to create the career or life I want in this constantly changing world I needed to be more bodacious." Mary wrote books as one way to get the message out, and to reach many more women, Mary had a website where you could buy her book, *Bodacious! Woman: Outrageously in Charge of Your Life and Lovin' It!*, read articles, and sign up for her newsletter. After her speaking tours, many women were particularly inspired and kept asking her how they could connect with other bodacious women. As Mary says, "This got me thinking. My response was the Bodacious Women's Club, which captures the main message of the book and continues to feed women's 'motivation meter'—all within the demands of their already active lives."

Mary's concept is to use the Internet as the central delivery system so members can access content and interact whenever it fits into their schedule.

The BodaciousWomensClub's business model is a fee-based membership club, with fees around $50 per month. It delivers the club-member experience by using a combination of a central online website, teleconference technology, and physical packages, such as inspiring CDs received in the postal mail. Mary and Cheryl say emphatically, "It's about connecting women. Not a pitch fest!" No matter what the business model is, Mary says, "What scares me about the Internet is that it changes so dang fast! Constantly making online changes, especially big ones, can waste time and money if you're not smart."

Both Mary and Cheryl stress that they are motivated by learning and trying new things. The journey, though, is not smooth or easy. Failure is a key to learning. Many successful entrepreneurs have failed in business at least once. Mary says, "I've learned that experimentation and failure early on is key. Failure and mistakes are great learning tools. My motto is 'Fail fast, learn, and move on.'"

Crossroads in Business.   One key to success on the Internet or any business is to know what your customers really want, and provide that. What your customers want is not always what you think they want. Listen to your customers. This was true for Mary.

In her own words, Mary explains, "I ran the first version of the Bodacious Women's Club by myself, and it was only for women entrepreneurs. I found three things didn't work. The club was not interactive. Information and ideas went primarily one way from me to them. The second problem I encountered was that it was draining doing it all by myself. I'm a high-energy person, but even I need others around me to help keep me going and doing my best. The third problem was that membership was dropping because I hadn't paid close enough attention to what my audience really wanted. Almost all of the women who love my "bodacious" message are in business, but only half are entrepreneurs. I was excluding half of those who were fans of my book, *Bodacious*

Woman, which is how to be bodacious in life, but not specifically for your career or as an entrepreneur."

Mary's challenge was to solve all three problems by making some big changes. The biggest was that she closed down the online Women's Club in order to think and regroup. Mary says, "What seems so obvious to me now wasn't at the time. All I really knew was that the Club wasn't working for the members or for me. Stopping helped me focus on my business rather than letting my business run me." So Mary rebuilt the club concept based on the solutions to all three problems. Give customers what they want by making it interactive, get a partner to keep her and the whole experience fresh, and change her market niche to women in business between age 40 and 65. That's when Mary invited Cheryl Thompson to join her as cohost. Together they relaunched the club.

Hard-Won Advice for Other Business Owners

From Mary:

- Be aware of all the wiz-bang neat stuff you can do online, but don't let what you think is neat dictate how the site looks or operates. It's so easy to fall into this trap online.

- Use surveys, send e-mails, call them up, and constantly keep your antennae out to what your customer wants. This helps you get it mostly right the first time, which saves a lot of time and money and attracts more customers in the first place.

- 80 percent to 90 percent of business is done through referral. Customer retention is key. Keep in touch with current customers. Grow your business out of your existing list of customers and prospects. Connect with them online through opting in to receive a newsletter or a special report. Also, connect with customers through in-person networking. If they are ideal clients and express interest, follow up. If you hit the right hot button, convert them to satisfied customers. Many women of our club are happy and refer us to their friends.

From Cheryl:

- The key lesson is marketing. You can have the greatest product but if you don't market it, you won't succeed. Small businesses struggle because they don't really want to market or sell.

- Many new entrepreneurs look for help from consultants, workshops, and conferences—which can be very helpful but very expensive. Be very discerning and strategic about the programs you choose or you can wake up one morning like I did, and discover you've spent thousands of dollars and have nothing to show for it. Base your decisions on outcomes: Ask yourself, "What can they teach me that I don't already know or could find out for less or free?"

- Look for programs that offer a satisfaction guarantee—100 percent satisfaction or get your money back. Don't do it if they don't have it. If it seems too good to be true, it probably is.

- Invest up front. Set up a budget for training and stick with it. There are many very skilled, helpful consultants and coaches who are affordable and can steer you in the right direction and give you lots of valuable information. Just remember, you are the one who implements the ideas.

David Riklan

David Riklan is owner of Self-Improvement Online, Inc., which is a self-improvement online publishing business that provides information, newsletters, and resources on self-improvement via the website, SelfGrowth.com.

David is not an accidental entrepreneur. From his first job out of college he knew that working long-term for corporate America was not for him. So, early on in his career he began searching for a way to marry his love of self-improvement and desire for his own business. Even though he was not technically inclined and Internet businesses were in their infancy in the mid-1990s, David realized that the Internet was his ticket. As many wannabe entrepreneurs do, he began by using the Internet as a hobby and then turned it into a small side business, part-time. After five years of careful planning, David took the leap into full-time, and he now has thirteen employees.

As David says, "I'm motivated by building something that's my own, controlling my own destiny, and having a positive impact on people worldwide. Yet, I don't want to do this alone. I love building a team, knowing that everyone is an integral part of the success of our organization. I'm following my dream of owning my business and helping people improve their lives. What could be better?"

Self-Improvement Online's focus is publishing good quality information and resources on self-improvement online through e-newsletters, e-books, teleseminars, and books. They cover three major areas of self-improvement: natural health (physical, mental, and spiritual), relationships (personal and professional), and finances (career, business, and money).

The business model for generating revenue is threefold:

1. Affiliates: Selling or promoting other people's products on a percentage basis on the Web and through their own e-newsletters

2. Online advertising

3. Selling products (books or information products) and services online. For example: One service is researching and submitting articles to online websites targeted to a client's market

The company's original niche was the "hard-core folks" looking to use the Internet to help them improve their life. They expanded and now provide a lot of information both online (Internet) and offline (non-Internet sources, such as courses, therapists, and coaches). Their mission is to give people the best information available to improve their life. Their niche is to provide quality, easily accessible information on self-improvement through the Internet.

Crossroads in Business.   David's biggest crossroad was turning his side business into a full-time business. As David explains, "After five years of working evenings and weekends, I knew it was time to leave my corporate job. This was a big decision fraught with risk. I had two children, and my wife was pregnant at the time. By quitting, I set up a no-way-out situation. I was clear; there was no choice other than to succeed."

In one year, David felt comfortable enough to begin to relax. "I could see light at the end of the tunnel—that our model was working." David's first product, an e-book, was incredibly successful. It made $100,000 in the first 48 hours and it still generates monthly revenue today. SelfGrowth.com is the number one self-improvement website on search engines, and it has over 900,000 visitors to the site per month. David also likes to help others: "Many people see me as a regular guy and are inspired by my success in the Internet marketing business. They can see that persistence pays off and that it might be doable for them too."

Hard-Won Advice for Other Business Owners

• Above all else, be persistent. Yet know when to shift gears—persistently doing the wrong thing will never get you to success.

• Take responsibility from the beginning and learn from your mistakes.

• Take ownership. Clearly know that you are driving the business. Pay the price (hard work, time, or money).

• Have a strong desire. Believe in what you're doing.

- Have a clear vision for the future. Set goals and create a plan to implement your goals.

Yes, the Internet is exciting and constantly offers new opportunities for entrepreneurs to grow their businesses. One person in a home office can connect and send their message out to millions of people worldwide. Yet this amazing ease of communication does not create international, profitable companies as instantly and effortlessly as pushing the send button on your computer.

CHAPTER 7

MAKING ROOM FOR MORE BUSINESS

Expanding Your Business

WHEN YOU KNOW it is the right time for your business to expand, ask yourself why. What's in it for you? What's in it for the business? What's in it for the customers or clients? Based on your answers and/or discussions with your partner and selected employee(s), formulate your vision for what your business will look like in the next two to three years and how you envision getting there. Now you're ready to set your revenue goals, objectives for business growth, run the numbers, and start researching what options fit your business and the vision.

Know when to loosen the reins. When you are running the whole business and all decisions are yours, it's hard to do let go and let others step in. But it may be necessary for growth. Often the founder of a company needs to step back and let her management team or her right-hand person run the day-to-day operations so that she can focus on new projects, products, programs, or the new expansion of the company. This is healthy for the growth of the company and ultimately the founder.

49 *"Know when to loosen the reins. When you are running the whole business and all decisions are yours, it's hard to let go and let others step in. But it may be necessary for growth."*

Some of the options for expanding a business are:

1. Hire key employees: A CEO, CFO, COO, Sales VP, etc.

2. Create a strategic alliance with another business owner in the same or similar industry in which you can offer expanded services that benefit both of you as well as the customers.

3. Franchise your business.

4. Open a new business related to your current business that serves a different market segment in your niche.

5. License your business and create a network marketing company.

6. Take on a partner.

Entrepreneurs love to create and try something new. They calculate the risks and run the numbers but in the end, they usually go with their intuition and their gut feeling and take the leap. I would like to share the stories of three entrepreneurs who expanded their businesses in interesting and creative ways.

Opening a New Business: The Green Leaf Platters Story

Hugh Groman started the new business, Green Leaf Platters, because he saw a need for it and a market niche that wasn't being filled. Hugh Groman Catering was doing very well and growing every year. Yet Hugh wanted to offer higher quality party platters with fresh food, priced somewhere between store-bought party platters and high-end catered events.

As Hugh says, "I love the stimulation and challenge of creating something new. I literally had about 500 people on my e-mail list who had called over the last five years but who hadn't become customers because full-service catering was too expensive for them. In 2006, I decided to fill the gap. The platters are cooked fresh and delivered just before the party starts. Orders are made via the Internet and we deliver the food ready to serve, arranged on white porcelain platters, and we do a quick set-up display. All the customers need to do is greet their guests. We're based in Berkeley and people are always looking for environmentally friendly businesses. So customers can also order simply elegant disposable plates, cutlery, napkins, and cups from us made from paper or corn. They throw all the trash into green bags we provide, we pick it up and it all gets composted. The price point is more affordable but still high enough so that we can serve fresh gourmet food in keeping with the quality and standards we're known for."

Hugh didn't want to dilute the Hugh Groman Catering brand by offering party platters under the same name so he decided to create Green Leaf Platters as a "sister" company. Hugh is the owner, but the companies are separate. It also became necessary to change his business structure from a sole proprietorship to an S Corporation. "This way I have created an umbrella company for multiple businesses. It gives me tax and insurance savings. The main thing for me is that the customer sees that the food quality is the same but the service and price points are different. We cross-promote. I believe in keeping it simple." The vans have the logos of both companies, the business card has Hugh Groman Catering on one side and Green Leaf Platters on the other. There are two distinct websites but they are linked.

Hugh's Tips

*   Everything takes longer than you want or expect. It took one year to get Green Leaf off the ground.

*   When rolling out the new service or product, pay attention to the details, pay attention to the way it makes people feel, and stay focused on quality.

*   Have a clear vision of what you are building, be willing to take risks even though it seems scary, take the wide view, and be confident that your hard work will pay off.

Franchising Your Business: The GoCar Tours Story

Alasdair Clements and Nathan Withrington started their business with a plan for franchising it in two years. They started with eight Go Cars, self-funded the business, rolled up their sleeves, and worked 24/7 to build a business that could be a turnkey operation perfect for franchising. They discovered that there was a lot of customer education required so that tourists would try touring the city in their cars. Alasdair spent a lot of time out on the street talking to folks about Go Cars and sharing how fun the cars are, while Nathan was taking care of the maintenance and audio systems of the Go Cars. People loved the little yellow cars and being able to toodle around on their own schedule with the onboard tour of their choice. Alasdair and Nathan were surprised but jazzed that GoCar Tours got almost instant press that has continued to spread around the United States and internationally. In 2005, they knew they needed to find an investor to help fund their first franchise. That is a story in itself but suffice it to say they connected with a private investor and took the leap into franchising.

GoCar Tours formed a franchising company in September 2005, sold the first franchise by February 2006, and another in November 2006. They are currently working on their first overseas franchise in Spain and another in Australia.

Alasdair Clements says, "Our franchise program allows us to expand by adding franchise locations rather than heavy investment in corporate locations. Given that vehicles are the main investment this would be very expensive. Franchising is a less capital-intensive way to grow. We still maintain ownership of the brand and franchising also provides a platform to cultivate our brand. Franchisees pay us a franchise fee and open the business in a city of their choice. The best part is they also finance the car purchases themselves."

How a GoCar Tours Franchise Works.   GoCar Tours earn 10 percent of all gross sales in the franchise system in the United States, and 3 percent on overseas revenue. The franchisee gets a professionally produced GPS tour built using GoCar software and a software license to produce more tours at any time. Also GoCar Tours provides training and support to all franchisees in the system as well as allowing franchisees to use their trademarks, such as GPS-Guided Tours.™

GoCar Tours are building a "GoCar GPS Tour Network," which has different types of tour experiences to offer, all broadcast by the Go Cars driving around each city in the franchise network. There can be branded content or user-generated content, where they encourage locals to tell their stories of their cities to tourists using GoCar Tours design software. It's a playful application of their software that engages both locals and visitors. Branded content is where they have a well-known sponsor produce a tour unique to their brand, which tells the customer what to expect when taking that type of tour.

Alasdair's Tips

● When you take a big step like franchising you can get frozen by fear or doubt. That's where careful analysis and consulting with experts helps.Ultimately, trust your instinct and go for it.

● Build a culture that survives beyond founders. It takes courage and no small amount of stress to take the challenge of doing a lot with a small amount of resources.

● Get and trust your own sense of your profitability; don't depend only on your accountant.

● If your business can be made into a turnkey operation, franchising can be a great way to grow your business and increase revenue without opening and running your own stores regionally or nationally.

Network Marketing: The Divorce with Dignity Story

Cindy Elwell hit a crossroads after being in the business for eleven years. Her business, Divorce with Dignity, is a nonattorney legal document business that provides divorce planning, facilitation, and legal documents to people who want to obtain an amicable divorce without litigation. Right now her business is very stable and has a great brand. However, it has saturated the market in the East Bay near San Francisco, California. In order to continue growing, Cindy had to think of other ways to expand.

She first thought of opening other offices in the Bay Area, but she knew that would be labor intensive and hard to manage. So she then thought that she would want to franchise and started exploring these opportunities. One of her first meetings was with a business consultant with the East Bay Small Business Development Center office in Oakland. The consultant was great, especially considering there's no charge for this service and the consultants are available as much as you need them. He explained that it's very expensive to put together a franchise—almost like taking a company public. He then pointed her in the direction of network marketing and showed her a website that offers these services to CPAs so she could get an idea of the process. She also didn't like the franchise idea as that would mean that all the legal documents would be done in a central location so clients obtaining a divorce would not be receiving any personal service.

After handling divorces for so many years, Cindy has found that each divorce is unique, and even though she is not an attorney and cannot give legal advice, she can refer people to attorneys and/or mediators if they need additional assistance. One of her competitors has franchised, and the cost of buying a franchise location from her is around $80,000 plus royalty, etc. So she realized that she can offer a similar service without franchising and enabling people in the legal community to set up their own Divorce with Dignity office and truly help people obtain an equitable, low-cost divorce that meets their unique needs by licensing the name and providing network marketing support services.

At first, Cindy was skeptical about the network marketing business model. But after researching it, she realized it was the best solution for her situation and how she wanted her business to grow. Cindy explained, "I feel each divorce is unique and I want couples to understand the process, part amicably, fairly, and truly have a divorce with dignity. With this model, legal professionals will be able to license into the Divorce with Dignity Network, which will supply the following:

* The Divorce with Dignity name and brand, and membership in a global network.

- If they wish to purchase additional annual support services, they can receive a website, the legal forms, marketing materials, cooperative marketing opportunities, mentoring, and training on how to run a successful Divorce with Dignity business, client referrals, and referrals to mediators and attorneys.

Network marketing will be much less expensive for people to set up than buying a franchise, as they will pay a one-time licensing fee and have the option to purchase the additional annual support services. They will also be able to purchase products, such as business cards, packets for clients, and brochures about the various legal issues involved.

Over the next five years, Cindy hopes to take the Divorce with Dignity Network global. In her first year, she plans to open ten to twenty offices, and then double the number every year. Cindy will step out of the day-to-day operations of her own office in Alameda by hiring a manager; this will enable her to launch, manage, and grow the network.

Cindy's Tips

- Do a business plan annually. Keep it simple. Review it monthly, preferably with someone else who does not need to be part of your organization, but you can both use that time to review your plans and financial statements. It keeps you accountable.

- It's also important to stay focused; it's so easy to want to go off and do new things—you're an entrepreneur so that's only natural. However, if you try to do or offer too much, most of your clients won't understand your services, which means they'll probably go elsewhere. Focus on your niche and do that well!

- Get expert advice and support from a business coach or an SBA small-business consultant.

- Determine your marketing budget carefully. Don't waste your money—track your expenses, and continue only those efforts that pay off.

- Provide your network with a realistic marketing plan. Emphasize networking and involvement with different trade/professional associations to make connections and get referrals. This is more effective and much less expensive than advertising.

- Provide excellent customer service—treat people with respect. You are there to be of service, listen, and help them control the outcome of their issue/problem.

- Strive to be professional.

If you are at a crossroads in your business and have researched ways to expand your business and devised a plan for moving forward, don't forget to re-evaluate, release, realign, and decide the best next step. It's time to decide if you are going to continue to implement your new plan or not. You have solid information on which to base an intelligent decision. If you decide to go for it, make any necessary changes and move forward. If you decide not to do it, you have learned a great deal and discovered new ideas that you may want to try out at a later date. Next time you are at a crossroads, you'll have a better idea of what steps to take and what method of expansion best fits what you are trying to achieve in your business.

How to Tickle Your Customers

REMEMBER THE TICKLER FILE—the original contact-management system? Use it or an electronic version to keep in touch with your customers, colleagues, vendors, and other referral sources. Whatever system you devise, however, you need to use it consistently. It's expensive to attract new clients, so you want to keep the ones you have. The 80-20 rule applies: 80 percent of your business comes from 20 percent of your customers. It pays to keep that 20 percent of your current customers happy.

Another thing to remember: One unhappy customer tells seven or more people about the terrible service she got at XYZ Company, whereas one happy customer tells four or fewer friends about the impressive service she got at ABC Company.

50 *"Even though you have happy customers, they don't tell as many people about you as they would if they didn't like your product or service."*

Even though you have happy customers, they don't tell as many people about you as they would if they didn't like your product or service. How can a contact-management system tickle and delight your customers, so that they love doing business with you—and tell their friends?

Build a relationship with customers by:

- Being authentic and patient

- Showing that you care

- Being responsive

- Not making excuses

- Delivering what you said you would, and on time

- Making it easy to do business with you

- Going the extra mile and giving your customers respect and more than they expect

Here are five suggestions for taking care of your customers:

1. To keep in touch, all you need is a good database and a contact-management system with all the "bells and whistles," which you update regularly.

2. Send thank-you notes for their business and referrals, and cards for their birthdays. Call with no agenda, just to see how they are doing. Set a goal of sending at least three to five thank-you cards per week.

3. Regularly send an e-newsletter containing useful information and news about your company.

4. Have a customer-appreciation open house at your business, with an interesting program and food.

5. Greet customers by name when they come in or call. Talk about something they told you about earlier.

Remember this: If you follow the simple suggestions above, your customers will think of you first when they or their friends, colleagues, and family need your product or service!

Hire Wisely the First Time

AMY JUST LANDED a large project. She already has several projects going and five more in the pipeline. After celebrating her success, Amy realizes that there is more work than she, as one person, can handle. It's time for help. In the past, Amy has hired part-time contractors to help her, but now she consistently has enough projects and profits to consider hiring one employee. Amy is tempted to hire the part-time contractor she used on her last large project because it would be easy and quick. However, she knows that the contractor's skills aren't exactly what she needs for her new project, and she has doubts about the contractor's brusque manner with clients. Amy has never interviewed and hired an employee. If you're like Amy, what can you do to get the best possible person for your growing business?

> My employees usually start on an "on call" part-time basis, then move to full-time. I look for people who can see the big picture first and then focus on the details. Staging is very specific and systematic and I can tell quickly whether a person gets it and can work efficiently. Organization is an essential characteristic of a good decorator. Other characteristics are high energy, intensity, adaptability, having a sense of humor, and being action-oriented. Surprisingly it is easier to teach design sense than the characteristics I just listed.
>
> —**Pauline Pearsall,** Pauline Pearsall Staging, Inc.

Ask yourself: What are the three personal qualities I would like most in an employee? It is a well-known fact that a large percentage of employees who get fired are fired not because they can't do the job, but because they can't get along with their co-workers, managers, or the customers. When hiring, it is crucial to evaluate a candidate's personal traits as well as their professional

51 *"When hiring, it is crucial to evaluate a candidate's personal traits as well as their professional qualifications."*

qualifications. However, personal traits are the most difficult to evaluate accurately. Above all, you and your employee need to be a good match, not only because this suggests that the two of you will work together well but also because your employee's performance and ability to interact with your customers directly affects the success of your business.

How can you discover if a candidate is a good fit? One good way is to prepare interview questions that help you draw out information about his or her business knowledge, personal qualities, and "people skills." These questions tend to be more open-ended than simple "yes/no" questions, and to focus on how someone has handled specific situations in previous jobs.

> I've been incredibly lucky. Often finding the right people can be serendipitous. I met a young man on a plane returning from Europe. He came to work for me, his best friend is now my partner, and his sister still works for me. I believe in on-the-job training. I'm proud of taking people with interest but zero automotive experience and turning them into master mechanics. In fact, a refugee from Laos who helped build our offices showed interest in cars. I trained him and now he is one of my most productive mechanics. I think character and work ethic are also very important. I want my employees to be grown-up and care about the quality of their work and take pride in doing a great job. I foster this by appreciating the employees, encouraging a team atmosphere and compensating them well.
>
> —**Michael Dennison,** Bavarian Professionals

For example, say that you want to hire a salesperson. Once you have determined the person's sales skills, you will want to focus on how they would fit into your company's culture. You may like your salespeople to be relaxed and casual, good listeners, relationship builders, and solid team players. Design your questions to help you get a sense of how good a listener or team player the applicant is. On the other hand, another business owner who is looking to hire a salesperson may be seeking someone who is highly competitive, autonomous, and goal-oriented. The sales person he chooses would not be a good match for your company. Here are some sample questions to ask a prospective employee:

- "Tell me about a time when you dealt with an irate customer. How did you handle the situation, and what was the outcome?"

- "What project are you proud of? How did you contribute to the success of the project?"

* "Give an example of where you came up with a creative solution to a problem."

* "What motivates you the most?"

* "How would your last supervisor describe you?"

Remember, your employee represents you and your company. Choose wisely.

When questioning a potential employee, emphasize what they have done in the past, because that is a good predictor of what they will be able to do when they work with you.

Interviewing Tips

* Write a job description that states your company's mission and what skills, traits, and qualities you require in an employee.

* Request a cover letter from the applicant so that you can get a sense of his or her communication style and personality.

* Ask each candidate the same set of questions. This makes it easier to determine the top candidates, because you're comparing apples to apples. In addition to assessing how well candidates answer the questions, listen to your intuition and pay attention to your gut feeling. Those feelings are usually quite accurate.

* Conduct the initial screening via the telephone to verify skill sets and get a sense of personal characteristics. Also, the voicemail message and the candidate's response time can be revealing. Invite for a face-to-face interview only those candidates who meet most of your criteria. This can be a real time-saver.

* Be an astute listener. It's hard to learn much about another person if you do most of the talking.

* Try to make the candidate as comfortable as possible. The candidate will be more forthcoming. Adversarial interviewing techniques to determine how well a person can act under pressure usually don't work.

* Note how the candidate's car looks inside and out, if possible. You may be a neatnik, while the candidate is a pack rat. Dissimilar organizational habits can create havoc in the office.

* Check references thoroughly.

Whether you're hiring your first employee or your fifteenth, it's crucial to find the person who's the best match for the job and for your company. A mismatch can cost you time, money, and business. It may take longer to find an employee who fits your criteria in the first place, but it's easier in the long run than trying to get incompatible people to work well together. Consider consulting a professional who is experienced in hiring to help you screen and recommend appropriate candidates, as well as help you hone your interviewing skills. It will be money well spent. Remember, your employee represents you and your company. Choose wisely.

Retaining Good Employees

WHEN YOU FIRST OPENED your business, you might not have thought of yourself as a boss of anyone but yourself. Now you have two or more employees in your business. The question you might be asking yourself is, "How can I get my good people to stay?" When you hired your employees, you did everything you could to choose the best person for the position. Let's assume that you succeeded in hiring two outstanding people, and that they since have become an integral part of your business. At some point, one of your employees might get an offer to work for someone else. You cannot prevent that person from taking a great offer; but you can make your employee think twice before moving on.

In order to keep valued employees, you may be tempted to find out what compensation they have been offered, then match it if possible. However, it's probably too late; you may have missed the boat a long time ago. From the day new employees walk in your door, you need to figure out how to keep them satisfied and productive. You may be thinking, "I don't have time to figure out exactly what will make my employees happy." Think again. The hiring process can be very time-consuming and costly. One rule of thumb is that the cost of losing an employee equals between six and eighteen months' salary; other hidden costs are lost sales and customers. It is definitely worth your while to keep those people who are helping your business succeed.

52 *"From the day new employees walk in your door, you need to figure out how to keep them satisfied and productive."*

Paying more money—compensation—is not the only way to keep good people. Although it is a very important factor, other factors may also play an important role, such as:

- Recognition for work well done

- Opportunities for professional growth and learning

- Rapport with colleagues

- Teamwork

- Casual dress and atmosphere

- Flexible work hours

- Family-friendly policies

As a small-business owner, you must offer benefits that are intrinsically valuable to the individual employee because, unless you have venture capital funding, you can't compete with larger companies on salary and benefits.

Here are some simple yet powerful strategies to consider:

1. *Ask your employee.* Simply ask, "What would make you stay here? What might lure you away?" You may be afraid that they will ask for something that you aren't able to make happen. They might—but at least you will know what they want and have a greater chance of coming up with a way to meet that. If you ask and listen to what your employees have to say, they will probably be very surprised, and pleased, that you care and respect them enough to ask.

2. *Include employees in setting organizational goals.* They will feel ownership if their ideas, inspirations, and creative solutions are welcomed, encouraged, and incorporated into the company goals. There will be things that employees complain about, but if they know their input is valued, it will more often be constructive criticism. People like it when their ideas are heard and considered. If the ideas are not implemented, that is usually okay—but the fact that you listened makes a big difference.

3. *Provide family-friendly policies.* What can you do that helps your employees keep a healthy balance between work and family? The easiest policy to implement is flexible work hours. You will probably get more and better work from employees who can come to work after dropping their kids off at school, or who can occasionally leave early to watch a child's soccer game or school play. Allow telecommuting one day a

week, if possible. There are many ways to institute family-friendly policies. It's worth it in the long run.

4. *Promote collaboration and connection.* Make your company a place where you can tell a good joke, chat with coworkers, and bounce new ideas off each other. When people feel connected, they enjoy their work more. Ways to bring employees together informally include: hosting a breakfast once a week; sponsoring a lunch in a park in the spring; or giving employees an afternoon off after a particularly great company accomplishment. Invite a speaker once a month to talk about a topic of interest to everyone. No one wants to be a lone wolf. If your business is a place where people feel free to be themselves and are appreciated for the work they do, they'll stay with you.

As you can see, these strategies don't cost much money, but they can make the difference between a valued employee leaving or staying with you.

Action Plan—What's Next?

NOW, IT'S YOUR TURN! Are you ready to take the leap? If you're already in business, where does your business need improvement? What new service or product have you been thinking about providing? How can you take your business to the next level? Are you thinking of taking on a partner?

Whatever is next for your business, set your intention, and use this action-planning exercise to start making it happen—one step at a time.

1. Research the Market
My next step is: _____

2. Do Careful Financial Planning
My next step is: _____

3. Find a Viable Market Niche or a New Niche
My next step is: _____

4. Do a Business Plan (each year)
My next step is: _____

5. Develop and Maintain High-Quality Products and Services
My next step is: _____

6. Implement and improve a Customer-Service Plan
My next step is: _____

7. Develop, Revise, and Maintain a Consistent, Ongoing Marketing Plan
My next step is: _____

8. Implement the Action Plan
My next step is: _____

Planning is essential—but nothing happens unless you IMPLEMENT your plan. Work your plan and watch your business thrive!

Your Business from A to Z

YOU'VE JUST LAUNCHED your new business. You have a great business plan. You've researched your market. You have a great location for your business. You've developed your pricing strategies—and you have a killer marketing plan. What else do you need to succeed?

Here are some helpful, practical tips from A to Z to help you grow a profitable, sustainable business:

A   Adapt quickly to changes. This is the "mantra" of the modern workplace. Be prepared to change plans quickly, even give up your pet ideas, in order to work efficiently and produce the results you want.

B   Believe in yourself. You are the idea and business generator. You make your business happen.

C   Customer service. Today, quality customer service makes you stand out. It's easy to duplicate a product or type of service, but not so easy to duplicate loyal customers.

D   Decide whether or not you will need to hire extra help to complete the project on time. Don't forget to add the extra cost to your proposal at the beginning of a project.

E   Establish connection with professional or trade associations in your field for contacts, referrals, and support.

F   Financing. Unless your business is a candidate for venture capital, it will be financed by you, your family and friends, and possibly your bank. Have enough money on hand to support a minimum of six to twelve months of living expenses to start. It's hard to grow a business when you're worried about paying the mortgage. For example, if your business is a professional service, it can take three to five years to make a substantial profit.

G   Give back to the community in which you do business. For example, volunteer on a local nonprofit board, donate goods and services to a school auction, or coach a soccer team.

H   Hire an accountant as soon as you can afford it. Know where the money is really going.

I   Invest in technology that helps your office run efficiently. Today, a home office can be as technologically sophisticated as one in a large corporation.

J   Jargon: Avoid it. Sell the benefits of your product or service without using overly technical language.

K   Keep it simple. Make the benefits and process of doing business with you easy for your customers.

L   Lighten up. You've done serious work to launch your business. Make sure you find time for family, friends, and fun.

M   Maximize your advertising dollars. Pick the ad venues that bring in the most business, and stick with those.

N   Niche your business. Create and communicate what's unique and special about doing business with you.

O   Organize yourself daily with To Do lists, a contact-management system, and whatever else keeps you working efficiently so that you can increase your billable hours.

P   Play at work. It's no mystery why start-up companies offer recreational facilities.

Q   Question constantly. "What works?" "What needs improvement?" and "How can I position this product better?"

R Remember the 80-20 rule: 80 percent of your business comes from 20 percent of your customers. Make sure you reach those 20 percent frequently.

S Support is essential, especially from your family. You can't do it all alone.

T Talk to your competitors. They're the best source of market information and trends.

U Use all available resources to stay ahead of the market curve.

V Voicemail. Make sure you have a professional, friendly message. Change it frequently as your schedule changes to let your customers know when they can expect to reach you. Return calls promptly.

W "We," as in "We would be happy to provide that service for you!" Even if you are a sole proprietor, using the proverbial "we" makes your company sound bigger.

X eXpect success. A positive, optimistic attitude is infectious. Your colleagues and customers will notice.

Y Your website gives you a national and international presence for business opportunities. It also can serve as your online brochure, which is quick, easy, and inexpensive to update as well as offering a shopping cart for sales.

Z Zzzzz peacefully at night. You've done a great job.

Index

About the Author

Like many business owners, **Susan Urquhart-Brown** never expected to end up as an entrepreneur. In 1995, at age 50, Susan launched her business, Career Steps123, in Oakland, California, because it spoke to her passion for helping people choose a career or business that truly suits them. She quickly realized there was a lot more to being a successful business owner than hanging out a shingle and waiting for the phone to ring.

This is why Susan wrote *The Accidental Entrepreneur* as an upbeat, encouraging, no-nonsense guidebook that takes the mystery out of running a successful business for small business owners in their first years in business.

As a business coach, Susan helps clients break through barriers and provides communication and negotiation skills, goal setting, business planning, streetwise marketing, and accountability for success.

Susan has 20 years experience in career consulting, business coaching, marketing, speaking, and training, and has a B.A. in English Literature from Allegheny College, Meadville, Pennsylvania; an M.A. in Education from College of Notre Dame, Belmont, California; and a Post-Graduate Certificate in Career Development from John F. Kennedy University in Pleasant Hill, California. Susan has been an adjunct instructor at Santa Clara University, University of California Berkeley Extension, and John F. Kennedy University.

Susan is also Vice President of the Board of Directors for Global Partners for Development, a nonprofit, nongovernmental organization that works in the East African countries of Kenya, Tanzania, and Uganda with projects that have included development of clean water sources, child nutrition, medical and health care, primary and vocational education, and women's economic self-reliance. Their mission is "Ending Poverty Through the Power of Partnerships."

Since Susan's 2004 visit to Tanzania, tips and techniques shared in a women's economic development coaching program have been passed among women in various fledgling businesses in Tanzania and Kenya.

Through her work and this book, Susan's personal mission is to inspire "solopreneurs" all over the world who want to make a difference by contributing to world peace. It is Susan's belief that when people love their work, they spread happiness and good will throughout the world since we are living in a global marketplace today. What happens one place is felt everywhere around the world.